THE
GALVESTON
THAT WAS

THE GALVESTON THAT WAS

HOWARD BARNSTONE

Photographs by
Henri Cartier-Bresson
and **Ezra Stoller**

Foreword by
James Johnson Sweeney
Afterword by
Peter H. Brink

Rice University Press, Houston
Published in Association with
The Museum of Fine Arts, Houston

e.e. cummings poem "christ but they're few" © 1963 by Marion Morehouse Cummings. Reprinted from *73 Poems* by e. e. cummings by permission of Harcourt, Brace & World, Inc.

Annotated reprint 1993 by Rice University Press in association with the Museum of Fine Arts, Houston

Rice University Press
P.O. Box 1892
Houston, Texas 77251

Originally published 1966 by the Macmillan Company, New York, and the Museum of Fine Arts, Houston.

Book design by Diane Butler & Associates
Printed in Japan by Dai Nippon

Library of Congress Cataloging-in-Publication Data
Barnstone, Howard, 1923–1987.
The Galveston that was/ Howard Barnstone; photographs by Henri Cartier-Bresson and Ezra Stoller; foreword by James Johnson Sweeney; afterword by Peter H. Brink.
    p.   cm.
Originally published: New York: Macmillan; Houston: Museum of Fine Arts, © 1966.
    Includes index.
    ISBN 0-89263-326-3: $39.95
    1. Historic buildings—Texas—Galveston. 2. Architecture—Texas—Galveston. 3. Galveston (Tex.)—Buildings, structures, etc. I. Cartier-Bresson, Henri, 1908– II. Stoller, Ezra. III. Museum of Fine Arts, Houston. IV. Title.

F394.G2B3 1993   93-44052
976.4' 139—dc20   CIP

FRONTISPIECE:
THE MCDONALD HOUSE, 1890.
Henri Cartier-Bresson, Magnum.

This book is dedicated to my wife

Gertrude

Here in Galveston the humidity was like a clammy hand held over your face. Yet the city had a ghostly charm. The scent of the tangled gardens hung heavy on the muggy air. The houses, pockmarked by the salt mist and the sun and heat and mildew, seemed built of ashes. Here was a remnant of haunted beauty—gray, shrouded, crumbling. What did they resemble? Of what did this city remind me? Miss Havisham, of course. That was it. Miss Havisham the spectral bride in *Great Expectations*.

—Edna Ferber, *A Kind of Magic*

Contents

Editor's Preface to the Annotated Edition

In his afterword to this edition, Peter Brink remarks upon the fact that, early in his search for a publisher, Howard Barnstone reached the conclusion that he did not wish to publish his book with a university press. There is a good reason for this: the book is not a scholarly one. *The Galveston That Was* is a haunting tale of a time and place long past, and, in all likelihood, Barnstone realized that the rather conservative standards of a university press might serve to dampen the spirit of the book as he envisioned it.

When we first agreed to publish *The Galveston That Was*, we thought it would be a straightforward reprint, but as the project progressed, it became clear that more was involved. There were a number of inaccuracies and puzzling omissions that, from an editorial standpoint, had to be addressed. The status of many of the buildings had changed since the book was first published, and there was the matter of an errata list compiled in 1977 by Evangeline Whorton of the Galveston Historical Foundation and Stephen Fox of the Anchorage Foundation and approved by Barnstone for inclusion in future editions. How best to handle the many updates and corrections to the text and still maintain the integrity of the original?

Our policy was to correct what were obvious typographical errors and stylistic inconsistencies. Updates and substantive corrections were best handled, we decided, through a series of alphabetic annotations; the only time we actually altered the text was in accordance with the errata list approved by the author. We hope the reader will not find our notes too intrusive.

The idea to bring the book back into print was that of George and Cynthia Woods Mitchell, whose dedication to the revitalization of Galveston is well known. It was the Mitchells who approach-ed the Museum of Fine Arts, Houston—the institution behind the original publication—with a commitment of funds to help with the reprint.

When Anne Wilkes Tucker, Gus and Lyndall Wortham Curator of Photography at the MFA, contacted us about republishing *The Galveston That Was*, we jumped at the chance. We had known of the book for years and were keenly aware that, though out of print, it was much sought after, perhaps now more so than ever, given the tremendous preservation effort afoot on the island, one that had matured significantly since its early days when the Galveston Historical Foundation purchased and restored the Williams-Tucker House.

In addition to the Mitchells, a number of people have helped make this reprint possible—Dancie Perugini Ware, in particular, for representing the Mitchells and spearheading the effort to promote the book, and Peter C. Marzio, director of the MFA, and Anne Tucker for bringing together all the key players and planning an exhibition of photographs from the publication. Thanks also to Diane Lovejoy, Kathleen Hartt, Maggie Olvey and Mark Petr of the MFA, to Anne S. Bohnn and Stephen Fox of the Anchorage Foundation and to Harris L. Kempner, Jr., and Edwin Eubanks for their support. We are grateful to Ellen Beasley for reviewing the manuscript and providing most of the updates on the buildings and to Caitlin Wood for assisting with the copy editing and fact checking. Special thanks also to the Barnstone heirs for their cooperation in this endeavor and to Xing Koh, Ryan Hess, Polly Koch, Michelle Nichols, Diane Butler, Michael Muhlherr, Virginia Galtney, Michael Keprta, Cal Stockton, Karl Kilian, Casey Green of the Rosenberg Library and Betty Massey and Olivia Meyer of the Galveston Historical Foundation.

—Susan Bielstein
Rice University Press

Foreword

Today in art, as in living generally, we are faced by a major imperative: the need to fight constantly against the steadily increasing temptations to conformity. The rapid development of communications in the twentieth century, the spread of popular education with its concomitant lowering of standards to bring them within democratic reach—the sentiment that all should be readily appreciable by all, whether an effort is made to appreciate or not—is at once the base and the evidence of this malaise. True art has always been the expression of the individual, whether across the stern discipline of the Byzantine icon or in the fluid, calligraphic idiom of the Australian aborigine. Quality in art is and has always been the product of a struggle of individualism against conformity. For that reason true art is our soundest guide and symbol in this growing problem of our time.

In a world where communications have cut down time and distance, regional art is quickly disappearing. An international style in painting, sculpture and architecture is practically inevitable—or perhaps international *styles*, one following the other in quick succession. In literature, as well, the local dialects and local color of expression, thanks to technological advances in the communications field, tend steadily to fade into gray *linguae francae* in various quarters of the globe, Hindi India, radio Irish in Ireland or an English that embraces the whole English-speaking world. Still, in painting and sculpture, in poetry and architecture, it is the individual flavor which gives the spice and vitality to expression. And this individual flavor is almost always the product of the relationship of the individual to his immediate physical or spiritual environment. This is the essence of individualism, and when this is given over in favor of an impersonal conformity, the struggle is abjured, quality fades with it and art goes by the board.

Regionalism in art is one means toward the protection of individualism against the total encroachment of conformity. Today there is no hope of avoiding an international language in the arts. But one way to keep that international language vital in specific cases is the protection, so far as possible, of the regional spice. Regionalism can no longer be expected to dominate any expression of contemporary art. But where it survives, dominated by the broader international discipline, it can give vitality to our art, as individualism can to our lives.

A museum's duty is to point out the expressions of the individual in his struggle against conformity—in other words to focus a light on individualistic works, that is to say, true works of art. Furthermore, a museum's duty is to record, preserve and set in proper relationship to the present the achievements of the past or of a passing age. A regional expression, limited as it may be by commerce and communication, as was already the case in Galveston in the nineteenth century, is an analogy in the arts to human individualism. And one service which it was felt the Museum of Fine Arts of Houston could and should provide in its institutional role was to record the quality achievement of its neighbor city Galveston during the nineteenth century before the monuments which constituted that achievement had disappeared.

The importance of this decision to make such a record is evident from the fact that many of the interesting buildings of Galveston—and one of its most important, the Ursuline Academy by Nicholas J. Clayton, Galveston's leading architect—have disappeared since the winter Sunday

Howard Barnstone first drove me around Galveston and we decided that the Museum of Fine Arts had a major duty to perform in focusing attention on this example of civic individualism of the Gulf Coast and in recording it—even the remnants we visited that day—before the Galveston that [was] no longer existed.

The Museum was particularly fortunate in finding for its undertaking two pairs of eyes of such broadly different curiosity as those of Mr. Henri Cartier-Bresson and Mr. Ezra Stoller to provide the photographic documentation for the record. And to have Mr. Howard Barnstone, a practicing architect with a deep affection for Galveston and a profound knowledge of its history and architecture, to bring together the documents in this first volume of the Museum of Fine Arts series of publications.

—James Johnson Sweeney

Acknowledgments

Most of all to my friend, patron, critic, spur and my strongest support, John de Menil of Houston and New York; then to James Johnson Sweeney, director of the Museum of Fine Arts, Houston, who engineered the project, encouraged me and made it all possible; to Wandie and John Winterbotham of Houston I am grateful for the encouragement to proceed with the book; to Mildred Robertson of Galveston, who is so knowledgeful of the buildings and the families who lived in them and who encouraged me from the beginning; to the late Tom Rice of Galveston, who showed Cartier-Bresson and myself—even on the day of his untimely, tragic and accidental death—the intimate Galveston he knew; to Mary Clayton, daughter of Galveston's great architect, Nicholas J. Clayton, for her help, her remembrances and her plucky spirit; to Ruth and Harris Kempner of Galveston for their warm hospitality; to my architectural partner and friend, Eugene Aubry, an ex-Galvestonian, for his encouragement, interest and patience; to Joy Peak, then assistant research librarian at Rosenberg Library, Galveston, who is responsible for much of the research material; to Charles O'Hallaran, then librarian and director at Rosenberg Library, for his warm welcome; to Miss Ann De Forest of New York, research librarian at Avery Library, Columbia University, for help on the Galveston Customs House; to Winifred Gleason, who typed the first manuscript; to Mrs. Hugo Dunhill, managing editor of *Interiors* magazine, whose keen interest has been invaluable; to Tom Daly of Galveston, architectural student at the University of Texas in Austin, who made available to me many of the original Clayton drawings; to historian Earl W. Fornell, professor at Lamar State College, Beaumont, and author of *The Galveston Era*, for his encouragement. He has led me to believe the work to be worthwhile. To Diana and Bill Hobby of Houston for their interest and their encouragement; to Malcolm McCorquodale, Jr., of Houston, who has helped in the business arrangements at every level; and to Marie Marburger of the History Room of Rosenberg Library. Then to Ruth Carter Johnson of Fort Worth, Texas, for her encouragement and interest. To Frank Wardlaw of the University of Texas Press for his enthusiasm and his special interest in this book.

Introduction

This book is about the Galveston that *was*. It is not about the Galveston that is; nor is it about the Galveston that will be.

It was not so many years ago that oleandered, Caribbean-like Galveston was the biggest city in Texas. By 1850 not only was it the trading center of the state, but the tempo of its trade, the success of its businessmen and the dizzying heights of their forages into architectural wonders suggested that someday Galveston would also be the great city of the Gulf Coast. "It was ordained to be the Seaport of the West, with a destiny of maritime ascendancy, of grandeur and of power."[1]

That this did not materialize is self-evident. Why it did not is another matter. Historians have long been concerned with the life and death of great cities, and Galveston is no exception. Why a city so well on its way to fulfillment should begin to show signs of stunting and decay at the turn of the century is intriguing.

The theories are many. Professor Earl W. Fornell maintains that, among other reasons, in the 1850s Galveston was bypassed by railroads and that "the Queen City was destined to remain a mere terminal of a spur line jutting off the main transcontinental line which passed through Houston."[2] However, New York City was also bypassed, with only two railroads entering onto Manhattan Island until 1900, while Albany, at the headwaters of navigation, was the hub of transcontinental lines and yet never achieved prominence. Also the railroads that did reach Galveston were largely completed by the end of the Civil War, yet her heyday continued for another fifty years, while Houston remained an ancillary center fifty miles to the north. So it appears that no strong case can be made that the health or growth of a city depends on its number of railroads or the amount of traffic that flows through it.

Furthermore, Galveston remained the real port. The port of Houston was not made navigable for large oceangoing ships until 1917. Sea merchants had no alternative but to go to Galveston. Had Galveston been seriously concerned with the threat to her power by the deepening of the channel to Houston, surely she would have reduced her notoriously high wharfage rates, or made some serious attempt to counteract the opening up of such effective competition.

Another theory is that the city never recovered from the devastation of the storm of 1900, which killed five thousand to eight thousand people and leveled much of the city. Did it so devastate and demoralize the inhabitants that they wanted to pack up and quit the city forever? Many did, never to return even for their belongings or the bodies of their families. But it is strange that we find cities that survived similar natural holocausts throughout the history of this country. The San Francisco earthquake of 1906 razed forty square blocks. The Chicago fire eradicated much of the city in 1871. These cities were rebuilt and they are now two of the greatest cities of the United States. The same spirit and faith were manifested in the rebuilding of Galveston. The raising of the city's level eight feet with Federal help and the building of the seventeen-foot seawall precluded another such catastrophe.

The life of any city is predicated on its banking and financial institutions, the acquisition of property and the construction of new buildings. In 1905, after the discovery of Spindletop, the first oil well in Texas, great sums of money and many facilities were needed for the embryonic oil industry. Galveston had the banks, the buildings, the shipping facilities, the port and the international representatives necessary to trade, both private and governmental. It had men with the necessary stature and power to package the oil deal and to sell Galveston as the obvious oil city. Yet it was to Houston that the new industry was forced to look.

At this point, the facts lead to a conjecture that cannot be documented and is unsupportable at the present time. It has been stated that at the turn of the century, a combine of Galveston's leaders consciously bottled up available real estate and financing and arbitrarily decided to remain the big frogs in the little pond. After all, life would remain sweeter and less arduous as they basked in their honeysuckle-scented gardens. John Gunther wrote, "Three seignorial families controlled it, and, to hold it within their grip, deliberately sought to keep it from expanding and competing with Houston, which presently began to grow rapidly. Today, it has been described as 'something like a fly in amber—not decayed but arrested.'"[3]

It is too easy to say that Houston businessmen were more aggressive in welcoming the newborn industry, or that they were simply capitalizing on the lethargy of Galveston. It was a conscious freeze-out. Houston wooed and Houston won. Galveston, the logical suitor, did not even bother to pay court.

Whatever these theories amount to, the fact remains that Galveston is today a small resort, well within Houston's vibrating orbit. Its decline, however, has left us with a treasury of the nineteenth-century buildings which, in most cities in the United States, have long since been knocked down by the swing ball of progress and renewal. The buildings are coming down now in Galveston, but it is the fire department's condemnations and voluntary razing by owners to avoid taxation which destroy them, not progress.

The cosmopolitan seaport of Galveston was second on the Gulf of Mexico only to New Orleans in tonnage during the last half of the nineteenth century. The late nineteenth-century Galvestonians felt secure in the fact that they not only possessed the finest deep-water harbor in the state of Texas but also enjoyed the power arising from the possession of the state's leading banks

and trading houses. As Earl W. Fornell wrote in the *Houston Post* in 1956:

The waterfront properties in Galveston prior to 1854 had been in the hands of several warehouse owners and shippers. On *February*[a] 4 of that year a wharf combine was chartered "as a semipublic company possessing a capital stock estimated to be $1 Million" called the Galveston Wharf and Cotton Press Company.

One-third of the stock of this firm was owned by the City of Galveston, the other two-thirds by private entrepreneurs of Galveston. *Some of the men which*[b] controlled the combine were M. B. Menard, Samuel May Williams, John Sealy, Henry Rosenberg, A. F. James, E. B. Nichols, William Pitt Ballinger, and the great banker Robert Mills. These gentlemen ran a closed corporation.

During the late 1850s, when it was fully realized that a port monopoly in private hands had been created as a result of the charter given the Wharf Company, energetic attempts were made in the public forums and in the courts to recover some control over the waterfront areas of the greatest natural seaport of Texas. The issue was finally settled in favor of the combine by the district court in 1869, when, with court approval, a "compromise" was reached that gave the city a few more shares of stock but no voice in matters of management.

Secure in the position which this court ruling gave *them*,[c] the Galveston Wharf Company began to take advantage of its position; the port fees charged by the company aroused ill will among shippers and Texans on the mainland.

In this situation Houston merchants such as T. W. House, William Marsh Rice, W. J. Hutchins, and shippers in general of the Gulf Coast area who were not associated financially with the Wharf Company began to look toward the possibility of developing a port elsewhere on Galveston Bay or on Buffalo Bayou. The "plungers of Houston". . . now began to look for an alternative seaport.

They were buttressed[d] by political and financial connections with the transcontinental railroad builders and in the possession of a *site*[e] secure from the hazards of inundation by stormy seas. Accordingly they projected their investment policies *along dynamic patterns*.[f]

They *therefore*[g] began in the early 70s, according to a contemporary report, to hire "scientific engineers to calculate" the effort needed to complete a "ship channel so that ocean steamers could come up to Houston as easily as they could enter Galveston Bay"; and as the last decade of the 19th century closed and the 20th opened they[h] had dredged a ship channel which freed them from the monopoly held by the Port of Galveston.

Houston now had a deep seaport of its own. By following a shortsighted policy the Islanders had forced the Mainlanders[i] to take measures that were eventually to deprive Galveston of its greatest natural heritage.

The leading Galvestonians were primarily mercantile-Southern gentlemen . . . who would have been at ease in the best society of Charleston or Philadelphia. Because they loved a conservative way of life they lost control of an empire to the "plungers of Houston" who, while they were perhaps as genteel as most 19th-century[j] Texans, were also rough and ready empire builders, who not only took advantage of the main chance but also literally created it with their own hands.

It may be illuminating to quote directly from a comment in the Galveston News written in the 1920s:

"For a long time, while Galveston was without competition, the Wharf Company had all the business it could handle, even under its own terms. The company built as earnings permitted. There came a time, however, when the pressure of business from the Southwest grew so great that Congress lent a willing ear to the cry for more ports."

And here is a later quote from the *Houston Post* of 1956:[k]

Houston is often referred to as a political port, but it is generally admitted that if the Wharf Company had shown itself able and willing to expand fast enough to meet the growth of business, politics would not have been strong enough to force the huge governmental expenditure necessary to build the Ship Channel. While new ports were building to care for growing commerce, the Wharf Company kept paying its stockholders dividends. It still had business enough to make a comfortable profit, but not, apparently, business enough to make the growth of its physical property keep up with the growth of business without pledging its credit more deeply than the company was willing to do.[4]

Immediately after the storm, the city of Galveston, well aware that another hurricane could totally wipe out the city, implemented the Federal seawall program by commissioning the raising of the level of the city. This is referred to in the text that follows as the "grade raising." It involved digging temporary sea-level canals into the heart of town in order to float hydraulic dredges that pumped hydraulic fill from the bottom of the channel in the port. This had the double effect of deepening the water and raising the level of the land.

Most of the trees and gardens which had been planted over the city's seventy years of rapid growth were suddenly either removed or smothered in salt-brined sand and clay. All of the handsome trees that one now sees in Galveston date from after 1903 to 1905.

Most buildings in Galveston had been built on stilts or high basements because of the ever-present threat of floods. The grade raising in these instances meant simply filling in around the bases of the buildings. Some structures, such as old Trinity Church, the seat of one of the oldest Episcopal parishes in Texas, were apparently too low to begin with, and the heroic job of raising the solid brick Gothic Revival structure on hand-operated jacks is still legendary in Galveston.

Downtown most of the commercial blocks had been built three to five feet higher than the street, both in anticipation of floods and so that their doors would be at wagonbed level.

For various reasons many important buildings in Galveston have not been shown in this book. To name a few: the Burr House[l] at 1228 Avenue I; the Heye House at 1226 Avenue E; the Marwitz Home, a splendid brick pile at Twenty-second Street and H; the Beissner House at 2813 Avenue H; the N. L. Ricker House of 1888 by N. J. Clayton; the J. J. Schott House, presently owned by Mrs. Austin, an important building architecturally; St. Patrick's Catholic Church by N. J. Clayton, still a handsome and impressive Gothic Revival building; the John Sealy Hospital of 1889 by N. J. Clayton; the original Sacred Heart Church of 1884 by N. J. Clayton; the Masonic Temple of 1882 by N. J. Clayton; the Galveston County Jail of 1878 by Eugene T. Heiner;[m] the

United States Post Office and Customs House of 1891 demolished in 1935; the famous Tremont Hotel; and the Tremont Opera House. Many other buildings which are now gone have not been illustrated or described.

Whether a building is illustrated in this book or not is no indication of its importance either architecturally or in the history of Galveston. If a building is not illustrated, it merely means that research material and old photos were too scanty to qualify them or that the sun was not just right when one or the other of our photographers visited Galveston.

Notes

1. Andrew Morrison, *The Port of Galveston* (St. Louis: The Englehardt Series, 1890), 4.

2. Earl W. Fornell, *The Galveston Era* (Austin: University of Texas Press, 1961), 192.

3. John Gunther, *Taken at the Flood: The Story of Albert D. Lasker* (New York: Harper & Row, 1960), 18.

4. Earl W. Fornell, "Galveston-Houston Rivalry: Object Lesson for the Future," *Houston Post*, 30 September 1956.

a. Italics added. "February" is author's interpolation. Fornell uses "Feb."

b. Italics added. Author interpolation. Fornell writes, "A few well known islanders of that time who . . ."

c. Italics added. Author interpolation. Fornell writes, "to the combine."

d. Italics added. Author interpolation. Fornell writes, "The entrepreneurs of Houston, buttressed as they were . . ."

e. Italics added. Author interpolation. Fornell uses "situation."

f. Italics added. Author interpolation. Fornell writes, ". . . along very dynamic patterns."

g. Italics added. Author interpolation. Deleted in Fornell.

h. Italics added. Author interpolation. Fornell writes, "the mainlanders."

i. Lower-case in Fornell.

j. Italics added. Author interpolation. Fornell uses "19th Century."

k. The quotation that follows is actually a continuation of the *Galveston Daily News* excerpt quoted by Fornell.

l. The name of this house was changed from "Alvey" to "Burr" on the basis of an errata list submitted in 1977 by Evangeline Whorton of the Galveston Historical Foundation and Stephen Fox. The errata list was approved by the author for inclusion in later editions. Corrections or revisions to the text based on this list are hereafter referred to as "Whorton-Fox errata" or "Whorton-Fox updates." Regarding the name change of the building, according to historic preservationist Ellen Beasley, the Alveys owned the house for many years, and it would have been known as the Alvey House when Barnstone wrote the book.

m. Whorton-Fox erratum.

THE
GALVESTON
THAT WAS

Galveston Greek

The Menard House, 1605 Thirty-third Street, 1838

The city of Galveston was properly founded by Michael B. Menard, a leader of the new Republic, in 1838, two years after Independence. Menard had gotten his grant by purchase from Juan Seguin, and the land consisted of a league (4,444 acres) and a labor (177 acres). Apparently many of the Mexican grants had to be reconfirmed after Independence, because Menard paid $50,000 to the Congress of the Republic shortly after 1838.

Menard first founded the City Company, a corporation older than the city itself, on April 13, 1838. The site of the city was plotted and mapped into streets, highways, public squares and residence blocks which were exactly as they are at present. A policy favorable to the permanent settler was adopted in disposing of this land, and after making liberal donations for public, denominational and charitable purposes, the company sold its lots on the easy terms of one-fifth cash and the balance in annual installments. Nine other "proprietors" were afterwards associated with Menard in a joint stock company of one thousand shares at $1,000 each, making a capital stock of $1 million. Subsequently, as its resources expanded this organization was still more greatly enlarged in membership.

By 1839 trade was lively in the infant port. In the first year 228 ships of one kind or another had passed over the sandbar at the mouth of the harbor with its twelve-foot depth of water. A hundred or so buildings were under construction, including hotels, houses and even schools. The firm of McKinney and Williams had emerged as a large cotton shipper. The latter member of the firm, Samuel May Williams, had a rich brother in Baltimore who furnished the company with capi-

tal, and soon the real life of the town—the shipping, storing and ginning of cotton and speculation in the commodity was under way in earnest.

One of the first houses to be built in what appeared as the building boom of 1838 is the conservative but fashionable Menard House (The Oaks) at 1605 Thirty-third Street. Built by the founder of the city, it was meant to be a showcase from its outset.

Galveston, in the late 1830s and for decades thereafter, had a peculiar problem in its direct oceanic ties to the eastern seaboard. Ships which came to pick up the huge cotton bales generally arrived in port fairly empty, as the rum, cloth, paper, books, pharmaceuticals and other necessities of the frontier could in no way match the bulk of the bale. Prefabrication of structures in the East was a shrewd solution to the empty east-to-west bottoms, and it solved the problem of the lack of skilled carpenters in the West. The Menard House arrived "knock-down" from one of the Maine ports, probably Bath, with studding, siding, columns and capitals all premarked for assembly and morticing in the Wild West. Did the columns, when they arrived, prove to be too short or, more likely, did the bases rot out? Whatever the answer, square boxes are set below the debased columns, and the result looks like an example of the rare and cumbersome Roman Ionic in an era of slavish conformity to the true Ionic with its elegantly low Attic base.

The Menard House, while not a brilliant example of Greek Revival, shows an air of standard competency in its proportion, and the central pavilion of four columns with attached wings is vaguely reminiscent of the Erechtheum. It is said that the house originally had a balustrade parapet at the roof line; this must have added a certain color to the sober scheme.

Lower-ceilinged than most of its contemporaries (8 feet 6 inches), the house has two stories with floor-to-ceiling windows and doors, broad porches on both floors directly off the rooms and wide stairways—all designed to permit the greatest possible ventilation. The typical raised first floor—often from three to as many as ten feet above the ground—provided some additional ventilation during the summer heat and protected the house from flooding during storms. It was in other respects like most Galveston houses of the time.

Most of these homes had walled gardens in front or at the rear, with luxurious hedges of oleander shrubs, poinsettias, bougainvillaea, palm trees, and other tropical trees, bushes, and plants. At the rear also were usually a number of small service buildings, such as stables, wash houses, kitchens and quarters for servants—in those days mostly Negro slaves. In fact, many of the street systems of Galveston were augmented by alleys lined with very modest buildings for Negroes or other servants and sometimes with homes for the laboring classes.[1]

The house knew many a brilliant ball—the first pre-Lenten masquerade dance was held there in 1853, an affair which later grew into the annual Mardi Gras, the pinnacle of the social season, akin to that of New Orleans, and only abandoned within the last few decades.

Menard died in 1856 and in October of 1860, his wealthy widow "was wooed and won by Colonel J. S. Thrasher, a former United States Consul at Havana and sometime newspaper man. William Pitt Ballinger, the attorney managing some of the Menard property, appraised Colonel Thrasher as 'a man of ability but also an adventurer in politics and matrimony.'"[2]

The Menard family owned the house until 1880, when it was bought by Captain E. N. Ketchum, whose heirs still live in it.[a] During yellow fever epidemics, it was used as a hospital. In 1892, plumbing was added for the first time; it was not until 1941 that gas-fire heating was added. Up to that time fireplaces and wood or gas stoves had been used.

The Williams-Tucker House, 3601 Avenue P, 1838

Samuel May Williams, of McKinney and Williams, successful merchants of Galveston, also began the building of his house in the boom of 1838. During the years 1836, 1837 and 1838, Williams was often away from Texas, and during those years the city of Galveston had come into being. Michael B. Menard and McKinney had been partners in earlier days; thus it was natural that McKinney and Williams should be associated with Menard in that "wild project of Galveston," as Menard jokingly called it in an early letter.[3] The three men, along with John K. Allen and Mosley Baker, were among the organizers of the Galveston City Company and were members of its executive committee.[4]

"McKinney made preparation to establish the business in Galveston. The firm's large warehouse on the northwest corner of Strand and Twenty-fourth Street, known as the 'Palmetto' or Williams Wharf, was among the earliest construction in Galveston."[5] McKinney was optimistic about the prospects for both the new town and the firm's business. During the summer and fall of 1838, he wrote Williams in the East:

I may now be considered to be anchored here [in Galveston]. Our prospects are far the most flattering of all the merchants in Texas for shipping the present year's crop. . . . The eyes of all Texas are now turning toward

THE MENARD HOUSE, 1838.
SOUTHEAST CORNER OF CENTER
PAVILION.
Henri Cartier-Bresson, Magnum.

THE MENARD HOUSE.
FRONT (EAST) ELEVATION.
Ezra Stoller.

this point and we will be able to sell an immense amount of goods here at fair prices. So that we can ultimately make something like a monopoly of the best business of the country.[6]

With Henry W. Williams, the rich Baltimore brother, heading the project, the McKinney and Williams' interests built the original Tremont Hotel in Galveston on the southwest corner of Tremont and Post Office streets.[7] Until its destruction by fire in 1865, the Tremont was considered the best hotel in the city.

The interests and enterprises of the firm had become so widespread—including large tracts of land, city lots and warehouses in Quintana and Galveston, sawmills, steamboats, dwellings, a hotel and the wharf—that McKinney felt that the company had too many irons in the fire. He proposed disposing of all other properties in order to concentrate on Galveston trade:

My principal object will be directed towards drawing our business to a point over which it can be guarded, and to protect Henry, and thereby enable myself to attend more closely to our business in Galveston which will be more important to us than everything else in this country.[8]

Following this line in the decade beginning in 1839, McKinney and Williams, aided by Henry Williams, built up one of the two great commission-merchant firms of the Republic. Consigned to them were a large number of vessels whose cargoes they were authorized to dispose of, furnishing in return a cargo of cotton or some other commodity. The *Ambassador*, the first English vessel to cast anchor in Galveston harbor, arrived from Liverpool in the early part of 1839 with a cargo of English goods and was consigned to McKinney and Williams. By strenuous efforts they were able to furnish a return cargo of cotton and thus started a direct trade with England and other foreign countries. In thus laying the foundations of a maritime commerce international in scope, McKinney and Williams was a decisive factor in the economic development both of Galveston and of Texas.[9]

When Williams built his house at 3601 Avenue P, he chose the Greek Revival style as Menard had, but his house differed from Menard's in that it was only partially of wood, having been set on full-story brick columns. It was what in Louisiana was called among polite society a "raised cottage." Although it was framed in Maine and shipped to Galveston on a schooner,[10] the building seems to have been only partially prefabricated. The structural pieces are of northern white pine and hemlock; the trim is hand-hewn Texas long-leaf pine.

That the house was precut in Maine for assembly in Texas is without question, yet there are strong influences attributable to the Louisiana provincial and, even further back, to French Canada and northern France. Either the carpenter designers in Maine had a keen eye for the locally appropriate, or the house was radically changed when assembled in Galveston. The Menard House could be a stylish town house anywhere from New England to Ohio, but the Williams-Tucker House has all the earmarks of the South and the bayou country.

The original ground floor was swallowed up during the ground raising of 1903–5.[b] It had included a large brick kitchen with a handsome fireplace, as well as a brick room for provisions. There is another brick kitchen or outhouse on the rear which seems to have been added within a decade after the structure was built. The foundations were the first brick structure on the island.

The house was topped by a gallery and a central cupola, which were also in the style of the modest but aristocratic houses of the Bayou Teche; these were lost in a fire in the 1890s.

The Williams family lived in the house until the death of the financier-patriot in 1859. It was sold that year to Philip C. Tucker who lived in it and in whose family it remained until 1954—hence the present name—the Williams-Tucker House. It is now owned by the Galveston Historical Foundation, Inc., and is open to the public for a

THE WILLIAMS-TUCKER HOUSE, 1838. DETAIL OF PORCH, EAST ELEVATION. *Henri Cartier-Bresson, Magnum.*

[12]

THE WILLIAMS-TUCKER HOUSE,
FRONT (EAST) ELEVATION.
Ezra Stoller.

modest fee.

A most engaging description of Galveston and [of] one of its important citizens during the boom years right after 1838 was given by Francis Sheridan, an elegant young Irishman in the British diplomatic service, who spent some months on the island in late 1839 and early 1840. He much admired both Messrs. McKinney and Williams. As a passenger on a schooner from Velasco to Galveston on February 3, 1840, Sheridan wrote:

The first that struck me was a gentleman apparently of about 40 years, attired in a frock coat made out of a scarlet blanket with a black edging, & picking his teeth with a Bowie Knife. In this unpretending employment was engaged no less a personage than Mr. McKinnie of the firm of McKinnie & Williams, the Barings of Texas. On further acquaintance I found him to be far superior to the general run of Texians & acknowledged by all to be a very honest, charitable & Worthy man. He has been the making of Galveston. Among other eccentricities of this remarkable man was one which I much admired. He never had any fixed hours for grubbing—always eating when he was hungry & drinking when dry. His Partner followed him strictly in the latter.[11]

Sheridan says nothing of Menard, but he had strong impressions about the physical setup of the town:

The appearance of Galveston from the Harbour is singularly dreary. It is a low flat sandy Island about 30 miles in length & ranging in breadth from 1 to 2. There is hardly a shrub visible, & in short it looks like a piece of praiarie [sic] that had quarrelled with the main land & dissolved partnership. There is also another small Island in the Bay of a similar hideousness and called Pelican I. by reason of its being colonised by nobody but the Pelicans.[12]

The Town is very irregularly built & extends or rather straggles for about half a mile along the coast the Houses being of wood entirely with a few exceptions of the better class & these only boast of a brick foundation of a few feet. These Bricks are brought all the way from "Bosting" as it is generally termed & fetch the moderate sum of 40 dollars a thousand. Several of the inhabitants informed that they rather looked forward to the probable destruction of this inflammable town by fire, as an event to be desired, as, they argued "those who could, would then build their houses entirely of Brick & with greater regularity as far as regards Streets." The rapidity with w^h thse houses are run up is inconceivable, & I will not trust my imagination to guess at the number built during my stay on the coast. . . .^{c}

The climate of Texas from all I can learn is in the Interior one of the healthiest under the sun—The Coast in the Summer cannot be so, & the Island of Galveston at that time must be very unhealthy, & require the greatest attention & caution on the part of the Town & authorities to prevent a yearly visit of the Yellow fever as in N. Orleans, to the soil of w^h city, that of Galveston is precisely similar. Indeed when the latter gets a large city as one day it will, it will be in every respect a little N. Orleans.

In speaking of the yellow fever w^h prevailed in Galveston in 1839 a Texian physician who has written a pamphlet thereupon, gives the following accurate description of the appearance of the Island & the soil of w^h it is formed. "It is but little elevated above the surrounding water, quite level, destitute of trees, & presents altogether the general appearance of a prairie. The soil is light, porous, of a darkish grey color, with a large admixture of sand as you approach the margin of the Island and every where covered with a luxuriant grass. Water of rather indifferent quality, but just admissable for culinary purposes may be obtained by digging a few feet in any part of the Island." The water for the use of the Tables in town & the shipping is brought down the Trinity river in Steamers. The Author proceeds as follows. "The Heaving of the Tide has formed a natural Levee along the shore of the Harbour of about Two feet in height & one hundred in breadth. Immediately in the rear of this Levee the land is low, being nearly on a level with the water at Middle tide & over flowed at high tides. Further in the rear the land is elevated & consists of a firm, dry, porous soil." I cannot say that I was so fortunate to find any thing of the sort during my stay in Galveston, but however, the Doctor may have been so let him proceed. (Dr. Smith's Pamphlet P. 6)

Now all I have to remark on this extract is that, the Stench arising from the soil on w^h Galveston, is built, after it has been soaked with rain or a visitation from Neptune & "exposed to the rays of ardent sun" is appalling. I should say that on such occasions I have a more offended nose than ever I did before—with one exception i.e. when walking through that street of Funchal in Madeira, where the

THE POWHATTAN HOTEL, 1847.
NORTH ELEVATION.
Ezra Stoller.

debtors & prisoners in the gaol, disturb the passengers with lamentations & supplications. Of all the smells I ever—however to continue, in addition to the water & earth & the sweats exhaled therefrom by the sun, there is nothing fragrant in dead & decaying oysters w[h] plentifully bestrew the streets, to such an extent indeed that one of the principal medical men attributed much of the fever last year to that circumstance.[13]

Powhattan Hotel, Thirty-fifth Street and Avenue O, 1847

When Rutherford B. Hayes, later to be President of the United States, visited Galveston in late December 1848, he described it as a "neat, fine town on a sand beach and apparently healthy—a glorious contrast to the filth of New Orleans." In a letter to his brother in Columbus, Ohio, he said: "We hardly expect to find another place so much to our liking as this in Texas. It is built on an island, is high and sandy, resembling Cleveland, only not near so large or rich, and is every way a good pleasuring winter retreat."[14]

The year before, 1847, there was built a fashionable but ill-patronized twenty-four-room hotel. A strange three-column wing of the building remains at Thirty-fifth Street and Avenue O. The year 1847 is late for Greek Revival in general but early for this style of architecture to be used in a building designed as a hotel. Even hotels in Europe had not yet received this sort of architectural elaboration, as it was not common there until after the 1850s. The first notable American example of the Greek Revival hotel, the Tremont House in Boston, was built in 1828–29 by the great American architect Isaiah Rogers. The Tremont House was also a structure of dignified grandeur, but of granite rather than the more modest wood of Powhattan. "With the publication of Rogers' monograph of the Tremont House in 1830 the hotel joined the prison as a type of building in which American influence was important, and it was not for nothing that the big new hotels of London and Paris a generation later, labeled their bars and their barber shops 'American.'"[15]

Colonel John Sydnor, the early Galveston tycoon and slave dealer, made the mistake of building his hotel on a site too far from town. An indication of this error in judgment is the fact that when Rutherford B. Hayes returned to Galveston in March 1849, he chose to spend two days at Galveston's Tremont Hotel rather than at the new Powhattan. The Powhattan was never well patronized and never prospered. It was for a time the private home of Colonel Sydnor, and his daughter, Columbia, was married in the building. "During the decade of the fifties, Sydnor, a former mayor of the city, not only operated the largest slave market west of New Orleans, but also served as his own auctioneer. His voice, which 'was famous through the state,' could always drown out the bid of an undesirable buyer who sought to purchase a Galveston slave of long and respectable residence."[16]

The hotel was eventually sold to a Mr. Bolton, who first conducted a school in the building but, not finding this a financial success, made it his home for several years. In February 1881, the building was purchased by the city of Galveston to be used as an orphanage. However, when the wealthy Galveston businessman Henry Rosenberg died in 1893, he left the city money for a new orphanage, and the building changed hands again. Mrs. Caroline Willis Ladd purchased the building from the city and moved it to the block between Thirty-fourth and Thirty-fifth streets, where she had it divided into three houses. The main house now stands at Thirty-fifth Street and Avenue O. One house was destroyed by fire; the third now stands at the corner of Thirty-fifth Street and Avenue R. In 1903 the main house was purchased by Charles Vedder. In 1927 it was the home of the British consulate. In 1935 it was purchased by Jake W. Oschmann and sold to Forest Dyer in 1960.[d]

It is speculation that the building once had the

THE HENDLEY BUILDING,
1855–58. SOUTH ELEVATION.
Ezra Stoller.

THE HENDLEY BUILDING.
DETAIL OF QUOINING AND
BRICK JOINTING.
Ezra Stoller.

RIGHT: THE HENDLEY BUILDING.
INTERIOR VIEW AT SOUTHWEST
CORNER, SECOND STORY.
Ezra Stoller.

At right, the Hendley Building,
seen across intersection.
Henri Cartier-Bresson, Magnum.

traditional six-column porch. From known records, it is just barely possible to get an inkling of the original plan of all twenty-four rooms, all with fireplaces. Like the Menard and Williams-Tucker houses, the lumber, brick and sectional Doric columns were imported from Maine. Its interior details are more refined than usual. When its part of the city was being raised, the partitions in the basement were knocked out and the house was left standing three feet from the ground instead of the original nine or ten feet. An east wing was added after the grade raising.[17]

The Hendley Building, Strand and Twentieth Street, 1855–58

There were some extensive business houses here in *the*[e] early days, the town was small, but everything going into or out of the State had to pass through it. The Merchants here sold good[s] to all the interior Merchants until railroads were built into the State from Northern and Western Cities. The house of Wm. Hendley & Co., who were agents for the J. H. Brower & Co. *line of sail packets from New York, was the largest shipping house.*[f]

I have carefully avoided dealing in personalities as those who were here in the early days were on the same footing and all entitled to the same notice, but I think it will be interesting to some to hear of a few of the old timers. The house of Wm. Hendley & Co. was composed of Wm. Hendley, Joe Hendley and John Sleight. Capt. Joe Hendley had nothing singular about him worth mentioning, except that he had such uncultivated taste that he always lived a life of single blessedness. Wm. Hendley (or Uncle Billy, as he was called) lived the same way from circumstances. He was a crooked piece of eccentricity, bent all out of shape—with one little withered leg. He walked with a very crooked stick and his chief occupation was picking up rusty nails and bits of cotton on the wharf to the amusement of small boys. John Sleight was an enormous man weighing close unto 400 lbs. He was also a bachelor, which is not to be wondered at.[18]

The Hendley Building is somewhat less colorful than the gentlemen who built it in stages between 1855 and 1858. It is a simple business block, Greek Revival technically, with its granite-faced ground-floor columns. Actually, the building, its designer unknown, is a strange combination of the simplicity of the latter days of the eighteenth century and standard mid-nineteenth-century American style. The elaborate cornice, with its brick range of small arches and projecting continuous corbels, suggests the mid-century Gothic extravagances already popular in Paris, London and New York. The brickwork on the Hendley Building is that extraordinary one-sixteenth-type mortar joint for which Mt. Vernon Street in Boston is famous. The separation between the four parts of the building is indicated by granite quoining in the brick. The whole building is tied together by its ground-floor colonnade of granite columns and lintels and its brick cornice on the top.

On the ground floor, the granite columns and beams are not Roman-like veneer but are solid. Herein, in this commercial block, one gets the strong impression of classical Greece. The scale is different, but the few chips in the stone suggest the permanency of Corinth, as long as one discounts the possible fate of modernization with aluminum facing or the even more likely swing ball of urban renewal.

The slender cast-iron columns used in the interior are early examples of the use of that material. Inside, the shutters, the huge windows and high ceilings are ideally adjusted to the local climate. The sidewalk canopies were equally adjustable to a climate of searing hot summers and rain-driven "blue northers" in winter. As in most Galveston buildings they seem to have been an afterthought, though they were not. There is none of the real integration of arches and building which one finds in the Italian cities of similar climates.

The Hendley Building enjoys the distinction not only of being the first pretentious business building in Galveston, but also [of] having been constructed at a greater proportionate cost than any other building in the city. Although appearing as one building, the block is really four buildings, practically identical on the exterior. It was built in four sections, the size of three of them each being 42 feet 10 inches by 100 feet, with a rear yard, in addition, of 20 feet.ᵍ The section on the corner, however, was made 43 feet in width, with the same depth as the others. Between each section, individual fire walls were built, as for single buildings.

Its foundation cost thousands of dollars. The sand was excavated to a considerable depth as the primary step, pilings of great length were then driven down in an effort to reach a firm foundation and huge granite blocks were placed upon the ground and piling. Over the granite blocks, a mixture of concrete and San Jacinto sand was poured.

The laying of the foundation was started during the early or middle part of 1855. Almost all the material used came on sailing vessels from Boston. "The vessell, *Geranium*, left Boston during the early part of 1854 for Galveston, having on board 900 tons of granite, 500 barrels of Rosendale cement and other building material. The *Geranium* drew eleven feet of water when light and was a fine vessell."[19] The depth of the water over the sandbar at the entrance of the harbor at that time was but eleven feet, so it became necessary to lighten a portion of the cargo.

The laying of the brick began in 1858. The brick was also imported from Boston by the Hendley line vessels, among them the *Alamo, Travis* and *Boston*. Every brick in the building before passing into the hands of the brickmason for laying was dipped by hand into hogsheads of water and thoroughly wetted in order to assure the proper curing of the mortar. The building was not completed until 1859. At that time the Strand, the street the building faced, was about four feet lower than it is now. The building was designed for use as a commercial block and was planned to have the ground floor high enough from the surface of the street for drays and wagons to back up to the sidewalk to take on their loads without any undue lifting of weights. The street was filled during the grade raising, however, until the sidewalk is now hardly below the level of the ground floor.

The old building bears some signs of the Battle of Galveston. On the Twentieth Street side is a good-sized hole in the cornice caused by a cannonball from a Federal gunboat during the battle to recapture Galveston from the Federals in 1863.ʰ Throughout the Civil War, an observatory was maintained on the roof of the corner building, from which the movements of the Federal gunboats blockading Galveston were noted.[20]

The Galveston Customs House, Twentieth Street and Avenue E, 1858–61

Until recently when one saw the old Customs House for the first time—a trifle shabby, but with the brick still painted yellow and the trim cornices, columns and entablatures painted white—one gasped a little at the handsomeness of the design and the massive authority of the building. Here was a major architectural effort. The design was in the full vernacular of the Greek Revival and the date of the building would appear to be the first quarter of the century. A closer look, however, would reveal cast iron everywhere—window frames, balustrades, dentils, columns, cornices, entablatures. The date is clearly mid century.

Technology in cast iron would have made all this hardly possible earlier.

In Galveston, as everywhere else, cast iron was, by 1856, an approved material for everything from steam engines to customshouses. Its predominance as a building material in the nineteenth century was founded on its fire-resistant qualities, comparative cheapness, simplicity of manufacture and tensile strength. It did not decline in use until the 1880s, when the steel frame was developed in Chicago.

What an important building in Galveston this customshouse must have been at mid century! It

ELEVATION ON 20TH ST.

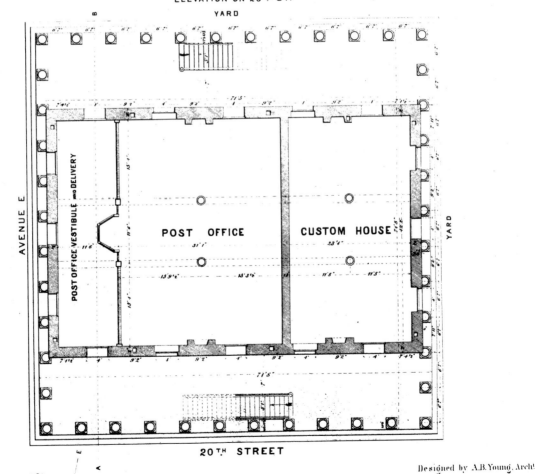

PLAN OF ENTRANCE STORY
Scale 8ft.=1in.

U.S. CUSTOM HOUSE AT GALVESTON, TEXAS.

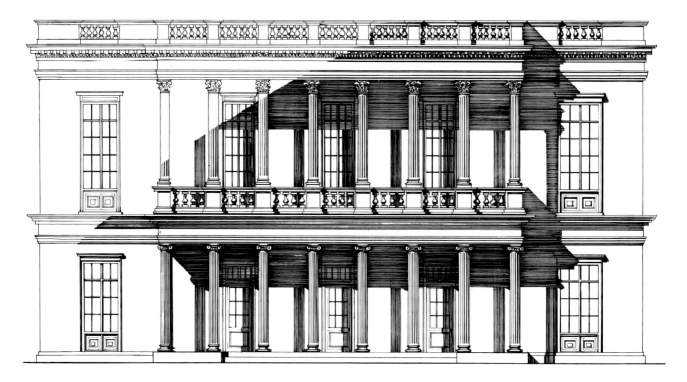

GALVESTON CUSTOMS HOUSE,
1858–61.

Present-day ink drawing.

was probably the first building in Galveston to have had an architect.[i] It was the first building in Galveston, and probably in Texas, except for the Spanish missions, with real architectural finesse and detailing. The story of its design and construction, however, is one which would send any architect to an early, well-deserved peace.

Intrigue, bad faith, delays and ultimately difficulties caused by the Civil War were only some of the problems met by the government in the construction of this combined customshouse, courthouse and post office in the five years from 1856 to 1861.

The great mystery about the building is who designed it. There are no cornerstones and no tablets for clues. The great government architect of the mid century, Ammi B. Young, designed a customshouse in 1856 for the same site. Talbot Hamlin's definitive work on the Greek Revival in America contains a sketch of a three-story rectangular structure, but this bears very little resemblance to the more pretentious structure now on

Twentieth Street and Avenue E. What happened to Young's three-story design? Was it too modest for Galveston? Did it too closely echo the design of the three-tiered Mississippi River floating palace? Was it too small and delicate in scale?

Among all the uncertainties, there are some recorded facts: The Treasury Department let out for bid on June 19, 1856, a set of plans and specifications which called for a three-story building. The firm of Cluskey and Moore (C. B. Cluskey of Washington, D. C., and Edwin W. Moore of Galveston) were successful bidders with a construction sum of $69,723.63 of "good and lawful money of the coin of the United States" signed on March 31, 1857.[21] From then on, Messrs. Cluskey and Moore apparently engaged in a great deal of activity over a number of years, most of it devoted in no way to the prosecution of the work, but to discrediting the plans, the site and the usefulness of the building—anything to wriggle out of their original contract and make a profit on a new scheme in which they would be able to work on a "cost plus" basis.

Even the highly respected Lorenzo Sherwood, in the words of Fornell, "lawyer, economist, writer, 'agitator' and political nonconformist,"[22] jumped

GALVESTON CUSTOMS HOUSE.
WEST AND SOUTH ELEVATIONS.
Ezra Stoller

GALVESTON CUSTOMS HOUSE.
CENTRAL PORTION OF SOUTH ELEVATION.
Ezra Stoller.

GALVESTON CUSTOMS HOUSE.
DETAIL AT NORTHWEST CORNER.
Ezra Stoller.

GALVESTON CUSTOMS HOUSE.
Ezra Stoller.

into the fracas and on March 24, 1858, wrote to the Honorable Sam Houston in the Senate:

Dear Sir—

We had an appropriation made some years since for a Custom House, P. Office, & U.S. Court Rooms at this place. After much delay, a government agent was sent out, who selected the site, which was paid for by government, and at last the contract let to Com. Moore & McClusky.

The trenches have been dug for the walls, much of the material brought on the ground and piled up. The site is central, and entirely eligible, and can be enlarged if necessary, and to any extent necessary, at as cheap a rate as additional ground can be obtained in the central part of the city.

It has lately been discovered by the contractors and some property holders operating with them, that the site of the Building ought to be changed and the building & site enlarged. The fact is, as the matter now stands, if the contractors went on and completed the building according to contract, it would be a tolerably economical concern; but there is not margin enough for much of a speculation. I heard an individual say a few days since, that we were entitled to an appropriation in proportion to the expenditure on the C. H. at N. Orleans.

Perhaps we may be, but if Congress wishes to do something really beneficial for us, we will be able to suggest something more important than to make an enormous pile of a building, when the one heretofore contemplated would answer all the purposes for the next fifty years. It is possible that Congress will be applied to for appropriations in making harbor improvements quite as soon as our commerce will warrant them. What we now need is the building, and the accommodations intended, and it is much desired here that the contractors should be set to work at it. Very respectfully yours, Lorenzo Sherwood.[23]

Notwithstanding the efforts of men like Sherwood, the contractors in November 1858 blandly submitted their new plans and contract from which the present building was probably built.

After still another year of delay, A. H. Bowman, engineer in the Treasury Department, showed his pique in his letter of November 5, 1859, to Edwin H. Moore, then in Washington:

Sir—

Before any examination can be made of your proposed plan for the Galveston Custom House, it will be necessary for you to furnish full details of every part and portion, together with complete drawings, on a regular scale, say the same as the Department's of one eighth of an inch to one foot. No examination can be made under such irregular drawings as you have now furnished, and they are herewith returned. They are entirely without the necessary details. A. H. Bowman.[24]

He had good reason for his short temper since the new estimates bore a figure of over $97,000. Two months later on January 30, 1860, Bowman wrote to Howell Cobb, secretary of the treasury:

Their allegation that it was not from any failure on their part, is an error. They contracted to complete the work by January 1859. This was two years after the date of their contract. With an ordinary diligence they could have completed it at [a] much earlier date than March 13, 1859, and if the work had been vigorously prosecuted by competent and energetic parties, it could have been completed in one year. The first story of the building is not yet constructed. This delay is owing solely to these contractors. The Department has not, nor has this Office, ever made, asked or desired, delay. The records of the Office prove the contrary. In this connection, I beg respectfully to call to your remembrance that in an early conversation with you upon this matter, in the presence of the Hon. Mr. Hemphill, I had the honor to state to you, that it was my decided and emphatic belief that these parties did not intend to fulfill their contract. The result has proved that I was justified in this belief. Both parties have been separately, for some months, offering the new and yet unexecuted contract for sale in the market.

The original contract was obtained by a bid, for a less sum than in my opinion, would properly construct the work. I so verbally reported to the then Secretary of the Treasury. The work was, however, given to them as the "lowest bidders." Immediately after they obtained the contract, they sought to make such changes as would change the pecuniary result. This they finally succeeded in doing, by changing the plan, etc. The only delay in this office was that necessary for preparing the new plans and specifications for the changed building. On the very day on which you authorized this change, the Supervising Architect took the matter in hand, and drove it to completion as rapidly as the work then in hand, and the force at his command would admit. They were sufficiently near completion for all practical purposes last April; but from various objections and delays on the contractors' part, no result was reached. All the drawings were completed last August, and the specifications could have been prepared in an hour but from delays interposed by the contractor, the details were not all agreed upon for more than a month. Everything (except the bond) was ready for their signature early in October last, but, though often requested, they have to this day, failed to furnish the names of their bondsmen for the Department's consideration; meanwhile, they have been hawking the expected contract in the market.

I desire to make no imputations against these gentlemen, but I wish to place these facts upon record.

Their next allegation is that I am in error in the proposed change for Beams, etc. This is simply matter of account, and it is not necessary to cumber this report with its details—it is a matter which may be well left to a computer. I am perfectly clear, and so are such of my experts as have examined it, that I am right. But Mr. Moore persists the contrary, with an earnestness which would almost induce the belief that it was his thoughtful conviction.

In regard to their offer to construct the work for the entire amount of the appropriation, I can only say it is for the Secretary's consideration, but I cannot, under any contingency, recommend its acceptance.

I have the honor to be, Very respectfully, Your Obedient Servant, A. H. Bowman, Engineer in Charge, Treasury Dept.[25]

Throughout the record of the long negotiations, who actually designed the present building remains obscure. Was this second plan the two-story rather than the three-story scheme designed by the contractors? The correspondence would suggest just this, but the finesse and sophistication of the existing building might indicate that another architect was hired by the contractors. Who could he have been? The similarity of the present design to a drawing for a proposed customshouse in Boston by Richard Upjohn of about 1825 suggests that perhaps a nameless draftsman was called in by the contractors with a safe and sure plan acceptable to the Treasury Department. Until more evidence is discovered, the handsome but stylistically old-fashioned building for 1858 must carry the attribution "architect unknown." It is entirely possible that the authorship was intentionally obscured.[j] All was finally settled:

It being evident that the interests of the Department were suffering by the delay, and that the unfinished building was daily sustaining injury, due notice having been repeatedly served upon the contractors, the Secretary directed, under date of June 18, 1860, that if the terms of his decision in regard to the contract were not immediately complied with, the contract would be awarded to other parties, and the next day did award the same to Cluskey's partner, Mr. E. W. Moore, who at once assigned it to the firm of Blaisdell & Emerson of Boston for the consideration of $4,000.[26]

The building now stands in fair condition, with its handsome *piano nobile* (second floor) cut up into ignoble spaces that cry for restoration.[k]

The Washington Hotel, Twenty-second Street and Avenue C, 1873[l]

On the surface an example of very late Galveston Greek Revival, the Washington Hotel is in fact a combination of styles. One first thinks of the eighteenth century, a moment later of Federal and then of the mid nineteenth century. It is difficult to believe that the Washington Hotel was built in 1873, the same year as the Paris Opera House. Where is the usual Victorian exuberance? There is no suggestion here of the Romantic Revival. Only the narrow proportions of the windows suggest anything but the austere dignity of 1825.

How did it happen that a building of this size

and importance was built in a style of [*sic*] almost fifty years old? Was it the archconservative nature of the architect or owner? Was it the innocence of the designer who thought style stood still? Or, perhaps most likely of all, was it the fulfilled ambition of the owner, who in his poverty-ridden childhood had dreamed of one day living in an establishment as gracious as the mansions of his youth? Whatever the answer, the Washington Hotel cements and reflects the love affair with the Greek Revival seen everywhere in the Galveston vernacular architecture of the time—the houses built by carpenters in what was known as the "Galveston style."

The influence of the Hendley Building is seen in the general composure of the elevations, although the ground floor with its succession of French doors and fanlight windows is a great deal more delicate. Its elegance indeed suggests an egress to a terrace and an elaborate eighteenth-century garden rather than to a cluttered sidewalk.

The structure of the four-story building is brick, traditionally stuccoed to look like stone, with floor joists supported on the exterior walls and on interior cast-iron columns. The sidewalk canopy, like that of the Hendley Building, seems an afterthought though it was built with the building. Galveston designers seemed to feel that a canopy was an unimportant or even an invisible detail and they never came to grips with the element, though it plays such a strong role in the appearance of the structure. Apparently the recessed arcade of the Rue de Rivoli was unknown in these far parts.

The Washington Hotel never "made it" as a large important downtown hotel. It had the mighty competition of the Tremont, the social center and prestige address. It seems to have been called briefly the Cosmopolitan Hotel, so as not to be confused with an earlier Washington Hotel, which stood immediately east of the Galveston News Building on the corner of Twenty-first Street and Avenue C. The old Washington Hotel was built, like the Menard and Williams[-Tucker] houses, in the building boom of 1838–39 and lasted with additions and modifications on the same site until it was destroyed in 1877. It possessed something of the charm of an old New England inn, and perhaps John P. Davie, who built the present building, felt that some of the success of the old hostelry would rub off on the new structure if the name were the same.

Mr. Davie died twenty-one years after the building was completed and willed his property to the Galveston Orphans Home. His heirs seemed to take considerable exception to this civic and philanthropic act and it was not until 1955[27] that the last of the lawsuits was even filed—this time by a granddaughter who died in the same year. In 1958, sixty-six years after the death of Mr. Davie, the case was finally settled and the building sold.[m 28]

Houses at 1312 and 1316 Avenue I

Galveston so loved the Greek Revival that long after architects had abandoned the classical style, anonymous builders continued to design vernacular Greek houses. The capitals of these houses indicate that the date of construction was sometime during the seventies. The flamboyant jigsaw caps are the only compromise with the era.

In the smaller houses with Greek fronts, the popular first-floor plan was a foyer with a stairwell at one side; on the other, two principal living rooms, one behind the other, and a narrow kitchen wing extending to the rear. An innovation that first appeared in America in the 1790s was the opening together of the two living rooms—front and back—by means of broad sliding doors. This became increasingly common after 1800. The Greek portico provided the equivalent of a shallow veranda across the front of the house and was sometimes replaced or supplemented by a deeper colonnaded porch at the sides or rear.[n]

THE WASHINGTON HOTEL.
INTERIOR.
Henri Cartier-Bresson, Magnum.

THE WASHINGTON HOTEL, 1873.
WEST ELEVATION.
Ezra Stoller.

THE WASHINGTON HOTEL.
DETAIL.
Henri Cartier-Bresson,
Magnum.

1312 and 1316 Avenue I.
Ezra Stoller.

Notes

1. Fornell, *The Galveston Era*, 93.
2. Ibid., 100.
3. Michael B. Menard to [Samuel May] Williams, 9 October 1834 (penciled abstract), Williams Papers in Rosenberg Library, Galveston, Texas.
4. Article of agreement (signed copy) between Michael B. Menard, McKinney and Williams, John K. Allen [and] Mosley Baker, 14 December 1836, Williams Papers; Ben C. Stuart, "Founding of a Great Port: The City Company," *Galveston [Daily] News*, 1 August 1909; "The City's Founder," *Galveston [Daily] News*, 9 December 1906; [Charles W.] Hayes, "Island and City of Galveston" (ms.), 261 [*Galveston: History of the Island and the City* (Austin, Texas: Jenkins Garrett Press, 1974), 177]. Letters of Menard and documents relating to the founding of Galveston and its financing are among the Williams Papers in the Rosenberg Library.
5. Hayes, "Island and City of Galveston" (ms.), 269, 285, 308 [*Galveston: History of the Island and the City*, 276, 383, 821, 829]; Ben C. Stuart, "Palmetto Wharf and its History," *Galveston [Daily] News*, 30 April 1911.
6. Thomas F. McKinney to [Samuel May] Williams, 16 July, 28 July and 30 October, 1838, Williams Papers.
7. Hayes, "Island and City of Galveston" (ms.), 293, 398; Ben C. Stuart, "Some Old Hotels: A Retrospective Glance," *Galveston [Daily] News*, 20 January 1907.
8. Thomas F. McKinney to [Samuel May] Williams, 3 November 1838, Williams Papers.
9. Ruth G. Nichols, "Samuel May Williams," *Southwestern Historical Quarterly*, 56, no. 2 (April 1959): 189–210.
10. Mrs. Paul Brindley, "Notes on the Williams-Tucker House" (prepared for the Galveston Historical Foundation, undated).
11. W. W. Pratt, ed., *The Journal of Francis Sheridan, 1839–1840* (Austin: University of Texas Press, 1954), 30.
12. Ibid., 31–32.
13. Ibid., 120–22.
14. C. M. Gruener, "Rutherford B. Hayes' Horseback Ride Through Texas," *Southwestern Historical Quarterly*, 68, no. 3 (January 1965): 354.
15. Henry-Russell Hitchcock, *Architecture: Nineteenth and Twentieth Centuries* (Baltimore: Penguin Books, 1958), 87.
16. Fornell, *The Galveston Era*, 115.
17. *Galveston Tribune*, 20 October 1934, 7.
18. S. B. Southwick, *Galveston Old and New* (Galveston: Ferdinand Ohlendorf, 1906), 6–7.
19. *Galveston [Daily] News*, 6 September 1908, 5.
20. Ibid., 18 August 1907.
21. Contract between C. B. Cluskey and Edwin W. Moore and the United States of America, 31 March 1857, National Archives, Washington, D. C.
22. Fornell, *The Galveston Era*, 163.
23. Lorenzo Sherwood to Sam Houston, 24 March 1858, National Archives, Washington, D. C.
24. A. H. Bowman to E. W. Moore, 5 November 1859, National Archives, Washington, D. C.
25. A. H. Bowman to Secretary of the Treasury Howell Cobb, 30 January 1860, National Archives, Washington, D.C.
26. A. B. Mallett, Supervising Architect, Galveston, to Secretary of the Treasury Hugh M. Culloch, 4 September 1865, National Archives, Washington, D. C.
27. *Galveston Tribune*, 22 November 1958.
28. Files of the Stewart Title Company, Galveston.

Notes 3 through 8 and other valuable reference material may be found in Ruth G. Nichols, *Samuel May Williams, 1795–1858* (Galveston: Rosenberg Library Press, 1956), xiv–xvi.

---

a. The house, which stood empty for some time, was saved by the Galveston Historical Foundation and sold in February 1994 to a Houston couple. Restoration is expected to be complete by the end of 1994.

b. According to historic preservationist Ellen Beasley, the grade raising began in 1904 and went into 1910; dates differ for different parts of town.

c. Pratt, 45–46.

d. The hotel is now owned and operated as a museum by the Galveston Garden Club, having undergone major restoration.

e. Italics added. Author interpolation. Southwick writes, "those."

f. Italics added. Author interpolation. Southwick writes, ". . . , line of soil packets from New York and E. B. Nichols & Co., Agents for the Pierce & Bacon line from Boston, were the largest shipping houses."

g. Beasley notes: "There is a reason why most buildings are the measurements they are: Galveston lots are 42 feet 10 inches by 120 feet."

h. The Hendley Market has undergone major renovation. A portion of the building was given to the Galveston Historical Foundation by Sally and Jack Wallace. GHF offices and Visitor Center and the Hendley Market are now housed in part of it.

i. Beasley notes: "Actually there were ads for architects [in the city directory] before the building was constructed."

j. According to Whorton and Fox: "The design of the Galveston Customs House has been definitely credited to one of the contractors, Charles B. Cluskey. Cluskey is best known as the great Neoclassical architect of Savannah, Georgia, where he was active in the 1830s. John C. Garner, Jr., when preparing the Historic American Buildings Survey for Galveston in 1966–67, uncovered a file of correspondence in the U. S. Court of Claims archive in the National Archives. Supplementing information already available in the Treasury Department archive, this documented Cluskey's authorship of the building. Donald J. Lehman recounts the vicissitudes of the Galveston Customs House in *Lucky Landmark: A Study of a Design and Its Survival*, published by the General Services Administration in 1973."

k. Some restoration was made to the Customs House in 1964 by the federal government. The building was restored in the 1970s, then badly damaged in an explosion in the 1980s. It has subsequently been renovated again and is being used for federal offices.

l. Whorton-Fox erratum. The following text has been edited slightly to reflect this correction.

m. George and Cynthia Mitchell bought the hotel in the 1970s. It burned shortly following hurricane Alicia and, after much debate, was renovated. The current building is virtually a reconstruction.

n. The houses have been renovated. One was damaged by fire but has been reconstructed.

VERNACULAR GREEK HOUSES
DESIGNED BY ANONYMOUS BUILDERS
ON AVENUE I.
Henri Cartier-Bresson, Magnum.

VERNACULAR GREEK HOUSES
DESIGNED BY ANONYMOUS
BUILDERS ON AVENUE I.
Ezra Stoller.

Galveston Romantic

Chapter 2 covers the era roughly from 1858 to 1870. In most parts of the United States it was an era of anonymous architecture. The individual architect had not yet come into his own. There were no architectural schools in America. The American Institute of Architects was still a small professional organization in the East. In the research for this chapter, the name of an architect does appear from time to time. But in Galveston, builders worked from handbooks and from catalogs of cast-iron fronts in the romantic themes common to architecture in the United States and England in this period.

The result is a potpourri of the styles and types that were sandwiched in time between the Greek Revival and the work of a single man, Nicholas J. Clayton, who was to take over in the early seventies as the architect of Galveston.

The Civil War interrupted the growth of the city. Nothing was built from 1861 to 1866.

Galveston was blockaded during the greater part of the War. It was captured by the Federals in October 1862, and was retaken by the Confederates in January 1863. From the beginning to the end of the great contest, communication was severed, traffic encumbered, industrial avocations interrupted, property confiscated, "the flower of the populace impressed for service," hearthstones desolated, and havoc made of life and happiness.

When capitulation was made on May 26, 1865, there was a general sigh of relief, and those who had returned soon set resolutely at work to repair the damages, and to resume the occupations they had formerly followed; so that on August 30 *Flake's Bulletin*, then, and for some time thereafter, a leading organ, said: "We cannot help observing how rapidly business is increasing at Galveston. The wharves are already crowded by steamers and other craft laden with merchandise. Old stores are being fitted up; dwellings converted into shops. All our merchants seem busy. Galveston is rapidly regaining her former commercial position."[1]

The J. M. Brown House, 2328 Broadway, 1858–59[a]

James Brown of Galveston could not have dreamed when he built his red brick Italian villa in 1858–59 that it would ultimately become the home of the Galveston Shriners. The Brown House was the first of the great palaces of Galveston. It was the first house to use the new cast iron, soon to be the hallmark of the Galveston palace, and it was the first house to depart from the deeply entrenched Greek Revival, which remained the vernacular architecture of the island. John Maass, in his *The Gingerbread Age*, gives us an eloquent and exact description of this type of house:

The Italianate villa was in vogue until the eve of the Civil War and this brief period has left us beautiful and distinctive buildings. None of the clichés about dark, gloomy, fussy Victorian mansions can possibly be applied to these high, wide and handsome homes. . . . Their ground plans are open and informal, featuring bay windows and sliding doors; the outward aspect is an interesting free arrangement of blocks and wings; the roofs have wide overhangs; the first floor rooms open on to terraces and loggias for outdoor living. All these amenities anticipate the same features in present-day houses by over a century.[2]

When completed, the Brown House was the first brick house constructed in Texas and the finest home in Galveston. It is one of the very few Italian villa houses in the South; the style, so loved in New Haven, Portsmouth and Philadelphia, was never really popular in the South. Immediately before, during and after the Civil War, when the Italian villas were spreading Mediterranean charm over much of the Northeastern seaboard, Southerners were usually too impoverished to indulge in such fashionable proof of having made the Grand Tour.

Brown was a successful hardware merchant who made a fortune in Galveston and was out to prove it. The brick, wood and plaster for the construction was brought to Galveston by schooner from Philadelphia, the original home of both Mr. and Mrs. Brown.

The main entrance extends the entire length of the building. On the left is the drawing room, completely finished and furnished in white and gold. To the right is a formal sitting room. To the north of this is the large dining room used for special occasions. As many as forty persons could sit at the table at one time. In the rear of the dining room, running east and west, was an immense informal living room (now replaced by the Shriners' ballroom), used as a children's playroom; when the youngsters grew up, it was used for parties and dances. On the second floor there are two rooms on each side, each pretentious and imposing. On the third floor there is one bedroom on each side. In the rear there is an annex of six rooms, two stories high, used as the servants' dining room, kitchen and storeroom.

Connecting the kitchen and servants' quarters with the stables was a long two-story wooden washhouse built in 1900. The stables consisted of three rooms downstairs and four rooms upstairs with stalls to accommodate four horses. The family was always partial to black horses and these, for the most part, comprised the stable.

Much of the original frescoing and plasterwork still adorns the interior walls; and the original panel French mirrors, extending from ceiling to floor, are still in place and in excellent condition.

The walnut valances over the windows in the interior were carved in Paris, and French artisans decorated the ceilings and walls in delicate friezes and panels ornamented in twenty-two-carat gold leaf.[3] Most of the furniture was specially built for the house because of the massive size and height of the rooms.

The rafters and joists are morticed and held together with wood pins. The roof is connected to the joists on the third floor with one-inch iron rods, placed at intervals around the house.

The walls in many of the rooms are covered with primitive—almost absurd—tapestries, the work of Miss Betty Brown, who was well known locally for her artistic ability. She had studied abroad for many years, and, since she had traveled throughout the Old World, she brought back relics and costumes from every part, which she sometimes unhappily conveyed to canvas.

Prior to the 1900 storm there were huge oak trees in the yard and along the sidewalks. Some were almost as tall as the house itself and were three feet in diameter. These were all blown down in the storm, one falling across Broadway and blocking the south side. The cavity left in the east grounds by one of the uprooted trees was converted into a fountain, which was thought to be one of the beauty spots of the grounds. The grade-raising operations of 1903–5[b] covered approximately three feet of the basement and grounds, as can be seen from the height of the present iron fence, constructed when the house was built.

On the death of Mr. Brown, the house reverted to Mrs. Brown and later, in 1907, on her death, to Miss Betty Brown and Mrs. M. E. Sweeney, her two daughters. On the death of Miss Brown, it became the property of Mrs. Sweeney and upon her death in 1927 was inherited by Mrs. Sweeney's daughter, Mrs. Henry Jumonville of New Orleans. The home was purchased by the Shrine from Mrs. Jumonville.

The house is intimately connected with early Texas history. It served during the Civil War as a hospital and haven for Confederate soldiers and as a headquarters for both Union and Confederate generals. Over and over again it is alleged in

Galveston that the swords of surrender were exchanged in the Gold Room. However, recent research indicates that the surrender actually took place aboard a ship in Galveston Harbor.

S. B. Southwick, in his book *Galveston Old and New*, says:

In those good old days there was much more sociability here than now. The town was small and all acquainted and much gaiety prevailed. On *New Year's Day*[c] most of the houses were open to callers and the male portion of the community did not forget to take advantage of it. The centers of gaiety on that day, or rather the *center*[d] of gravity were the beautiful residences of *General*[e] E. B. Nichols, who lived on Broadway where the palatial Sealy house now stands, and the magnificent home of Mrs. J. M. *Brown; the General*[f] was the champion dispenser of hospitality. His friends were not only expected, but required to drop in there about midday and help unload his groaning tables. Then those who were able to, adjourned to the other attraction, which was Mrs. J. M. *Brown's*[g] where they found everything as beautiful, lovely and entertaining as they could wish. Those who called there were expected to attend her magnificent Ball that night.[4]

The Salvation Army Building, 302 Twenty-third Street, 1858 (Demolished 1962)

This building, erected about 1858 by E. S. Wood & Sons as a warehouse, was almost unique even for the period, an era when the Galveston Chamber of Commerce tried to persuade the owners of all businesses to put iron fronts on their buildings. Until its demolition in 1962, it stood on the corner of Twenty-third Street and Avenue C. The design of the cast-iron front is unmistakably similar to the store in Philadelphia of 1858 for Dale, Ross & Withers by the little-known architect Stephen D. Button. It must be presumed that the builders' foundry in Philadelphia, Sanson & Farrand, sold the designs of the Philadelphia architect around the country.

In Galveston in 1858, Mechanic Street, or Avenue C, at Twenty-third Street was the very heart of town. The building was erected on that corner. The strange idea of facing the iron front of the building toward Twenty-third, the lesser street, with an exposed-brick side wall toward Mechanic, the major street, indicates that no local architect was involved.

As a result of this mistake in orientation the afternoon sun beat in on the west windows, presenting a serious problem, for which an ingenious and happy solution was found. Wood pull-down shutters were fitted to all the windows of the west front. Of all current sunshade devices, whether outside louvers or grills, inside drapery or venetian blinds, none seems to have such a direct approach to the problem of solar heat entering a building. Here is a solution that works under any sun condition.

The architecture of the front would have baffled any period-oriented student of style. There was the colonnade of Corinthian columns on the ground floor, topped with a Florentine running arcade. In and between the arches was a profusion of garlands and architectural vocabulary of classical sorts all stamped out with a great feeling of luxury. The look of the three upper levels was a no-nonsense expression of each floor. There was very little of the "striving for horizontality or verticality" that has plagued the façade designer from about this period until our own. There were no applied devices or tricks to make it look higher, or to make it "soar." If anything, the upper three floors had a vague suggestion of the Romanesque of Pisa, but even that was well integrated into the mid-nineteenth-century style. Perhaps, one can say, the succession of running arcades looked like a portion of a four-tiered Roman aqueduct covered with flowers. One can say with assurance that the loss of the building to the wrecker in July 1962

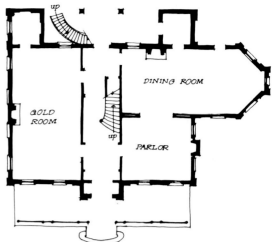

FIRST-FLOOR PLAN

THE J.M. BROWN RESIDENCE.

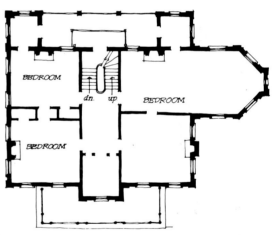

SECOND-FLOOR PLAN

THE J.M. BROWN RESIDENCE,
1858–59.
Ezra Stoller.

THE J.M. BROWN RESIDENCE.
*Photograph circa 1903 during
grade-raising operations.*

THE J.M. BROWN RESIDENCE.
DETAIL OF CAST IRON ON PORCH.
Ezra Stoller.

LEFT: THE J.M. BROWN RESIDENCE.
DETAIL OF FRONT-GATE POST.
Henri Cartier-Bresson, Magnum.

THE DALE, ROSS & WITHERS
BUILDING IN PHILADELPHIA, 1858,
BY STEPHEN D. BUTTON—
STARTLINGLY SIMILAR TO
GALVESTON'S SALVATION ARMY
BUILDING.
Lithograph by John Frampton Watson
(35 x 22½ inches).

LEFT: THE SALVATION ARMY
BUILDING, 1858.
Henri Cartier-Bresson, Magnum.

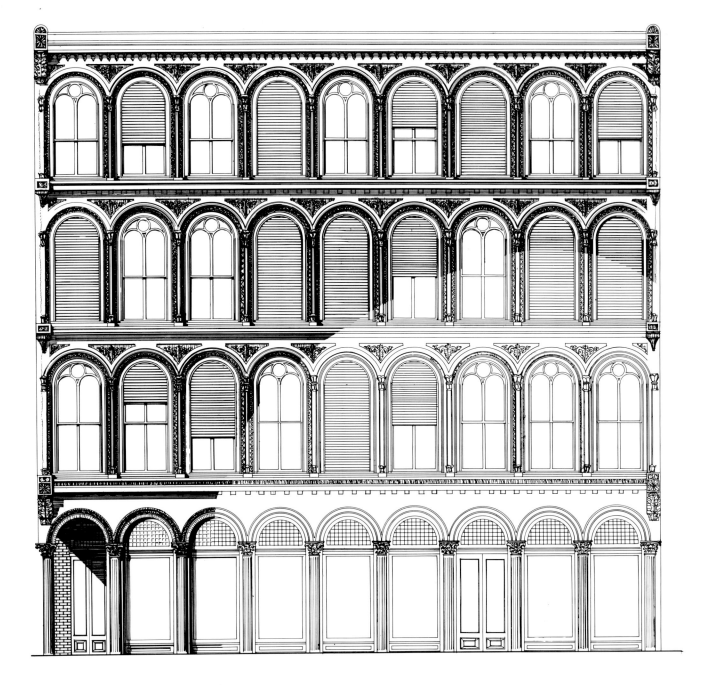

THE SALVATION ARMY BUILDING.
SKETCH SHOWS THE BUILDING AS IT
WAS LAST SEEN, WITH ITS PULL-
DOWN SHUTTERS. THE ARCHED
STREET-NUMBER CORNICES AND
INTERIOR CORBELS HAD BEEN
REMOVED.
Present-day ink drawing.

was the loss of one of the most handsome of the American iron fronts and the loss of one of the last buildings which can be attributed, if only in part, to Stephen D. Button.

The building was occupied at one time or another by many of the well-known commercial firms of Galveston in its nineteenth-century heyday. Its final occupant was the Salvation Army, by which name it was last known and admired until demolished in 1962.

Henry's Bookstore, 2217 Avenue D, 1858 (Demolished 1964)

One of the most luscious of the iron fronts to be built anywhere is the building which, until the summer of 1963, was occupied by Henry's Bookstore. Actually, the building was built for the famed Galveston publisher Willard Richardson in 1858 by a contractor, Mr. F. Brown. Richardson used the building as an interim plant for the *Galveston [Daily] News*, until the *News* moved into its large new building in 1884.

For many years the building housed the job printing, newspaper and press departments of the *News*. The first web press ever introduced in Texas was set up there in the late seventies. At one time, about 1869–70, the ground floor was occupied by the dry goods firm of Arnold & Brothers, and one of the most sensational burglaries in the history of Galveston occurred there, the burglars being chased by the police as far west along the coast as Indianola.

The building apparently remained in the Richardson family until 1945, when it was sold by Richardson's son-in-law, Dr. Willard R. Cooke, to Henry Ferwerda, who maintained the well-known bookstore in the building from 1945 to 1963. An earlier bookstore, Purdy's, had occupied the building from 1909 until 1930.

The iron front for Richardson's building came from the Philadelphia foundry owned by Sanson & Farrand, and the *Galveston [Tri-]Weekly News* of October 26, 1858, carried the following advertisement:

Builders' Foundry, Philadelphia. Iron Fronts and Building work, in all its varieties, furnished at the shortest notice. Also, Mettam's Patent Revolving Iron Shutters, castings and Machinery, and Jobbing of all kinds. The undersigned are prepared to furnish, at the shortest notice, Iron Fronts of any design, with or without Mettam's Patent Revolving Iron Shutters, a new and superior article. Girders, of all kinds and sizes. Columns, Shutter Boxes and Lintels, Ornamental Window Heads and Sills, Caps and Bases for Pilasters and Columns, Brackets for Cornices, Enriched Mouldings and Ornaments, and Every Variety of Builders' Cast Iron Work. They would refer to E. S. Wood, Ball, Hutchings & Company, H. Rosenberg, and Richardson & Company, Galveston; L. P. Blair & Company, Baltimore; A. J. Bowers, Richmond, Virginia, J. K. Goodwin and Brothers, Selma, Alabama, and to Architects and Builders generally throughout the United States. Estimates furnished to parties applying personally or by letter. Sanson & Farrand, Corner of 12th and Willow Streets, Philadelphia. E. S. Wood, Agent, Galveston.[h]

Commercial Blocks, Strand (south side) between Twenty-third and Twenty-fourth streets, early 1870s

Galveston perhaps recovered quicker from the ravages of the Civil War than any other city in the South. There had been a strong movement in the city against secession; Sam Houston had come to Galveston shortly before the legislative debate on secession and had pleaded his cause against secession well. The merchants of this commercial port bought and sold in the Eastern centers and Galvestonians knew Northerners in every phase of business. Another factor that probably led to some disenchantment with the "Old Cause" was that the Confederacy considered Galveston expendable and indefensible from the start and made little attempt to defend it against the Federal blockade and occupation.

Furthermore, slaves had not been a major economic factor in this mercantile society, even though Galveston had had the largest slave market in the state. In fact, Galvestonians had a tendency to spoil [sic] their slaves, and it became the fashion for rich people to try to outdo one another in the costumes their slaves wore on the streets in town. It is small wonder that when the war was over Galvestonians picked up where they had left off, totally undaunted and ready for more business.[i]

Galveston remained under a mild military jurisdiction until 1871. The governor exercised appointive power until 1873, when the citizens elected a mayor and adopted a new charter suited to the metropolitan development of the city. In 1860 the population had been 6,537, the aggregate business $8,992,000; by 1870, when most Southern cities were in a sharp decline, Galveston's population had jumped to 13,898 and its aggregate business to $18,320,000. By 1880 the population had soared to 22,224, and business had almost doubled to a figure of $30,308,000.

By the 1870s, Galveston had become the Gulf terminal of two great continental railroad systems, the Missouri Pacific and the Atchison, Topeka and Santa Fe. The first trains had entered the city with the completion of the bridge across Offat's Bayou in 1860.

The two sandbars known as the outer and inner bars had, from the beginning, been an obstacle in the development of the harbor. The inner bar is said to have been unknown prior to 1850. After its formation, the channel continued to shoal until 1866, when there was only nine feet of water over it. The city promptly appropriated $200,000, and the work, a system of piling, added an extra three feet of water. The twelve-foot depth was maintained until the great storm of 1875, which cut a new channel. In 1877 this channel was reported to clear twenty-one feet at mean low tide.[5]

In the seventies, the Strand between Twenty-second and Twenty-fifth streets was the heart of town. It now has long passed its peak, and the remaining buildings are almost all empty warehouses. The neglected cast iron, corroding from the salt atmosphere, adds an even more poignant note of decay.

The cast-iron front had run its course of popularity by the 1870s. In these commercial blocks, the cast iron on the Strand side was used only on the ground floor, where the passerby could more readily appreciate the wealth of detail. There, partial fronts were practically stamped metal, merely a façade for a brick structure. The buildings themselves are not particularly distinguished, but they exhibit the standard tastes of the 1870s. They have the slate-topped mansard roofs, which proved so disastrous in the 1900 storm—pieces of loose slate were a major cause of death and injury during the height of the hurricane, and slate roofing has since been forbidden by statute in Galveston.

These commercial blocks, like commercial building in all cities of America and England, were not precisely defined as to use and probably had no architects.[j] These late mid-century commercial buildings are all very much the same, as everything was subordinated to the needs of business. Such buildings consisted of a succession of identical upper stories, subdivided into offices or storerooms, with or without shops or representational premises below. The prosperous bank or insurance company, to whom prestige became increasingly important, was the first to seek dignity and architectural display by employing architects of established reputation. But this was not to happen until the next decade.

2217 AVENUE D, 1858. BUILT AS AN INTERIM PLANT FOR THE *GALVESTON NEWS*, KNOWN MORE RECENTLY AS HENRY'S BOOKSTORE.
Henri Cartier-Bresson, Magnum.

2217 AVENUE D.
Ezra Stoller.

COMMERCIAL BLOCK, SOUTH SIDE
STRAND, EARLY 1870S.
Henri Cartier-Bresson, Magnum.

LEFT: 2217 AVENUE D.
Ezra Stoller.

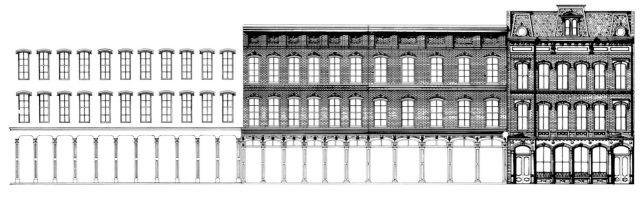

COMMERCIAL BLOCKS, SOUTH SIDE
STRAND.
Henri Cartier-Bresson, Magnum.

COMMERCIAL BLOCKS, SOUTH SIDE
STRAND.
Present-day ink drawing.

Today, on a walk or drive down the Strand, where only half the buildings are standing—oddly reminiscent of London after the blitz—one still gathers a strange impression of the vitality and wealth of business in Galveston in the seventies.

The Strand never achieved the urban quality of the Avenue de l'Opéra with its continuous cornice; however, it came as close to this sense of city as anything in Texas and probably as anything in the West.

The Austin-Fox House, 1502 Avenue D, 1868–71

As we have earlier noted, Galveston was one of the few cities in the South with a post–Civil War prosperity. In Galveston, probably more than anywhere in the South, the Greek Revival continued in much the same spirit as the "grand manner" prewar houses that had been built on both banks of the Mississippi. However, in Galveston the Greek Revival came into conflict with the Victorian taste of the late sixties. This house attempted to reconcile both tastes.

Galveston never really took the magnificence of imported styles to heart. What Galveston liked best was the strict orderliness of the Greek Revival, modified as Victorian taste demanded with scrollwork jigsaw cuts, corbels and projecting eaves. From 1868 to 1871 Edward Taylor Austin, an attorney and cousin of Stephen F. Austin, built this small wood palace. It was a fine example of the Galveston style, and it set the pattern in more modest houses for the great building boom in the decades to follow.

The Austin House, as it was known because of the long tenure by the family, owes some of its charm to its plantation look amidst city surroundings. Though now hemmed in by more recent structures, the grounds, planted with beautiful trees and shrubs, are ample enough to convey the illusion of a country house.

This property came into the Austin family in 1867, when it was purchased from Lorenzo Sherwood by Edward Taylor Austin, who served as a city alderman in 1870. The price paid by Austin, $6,400, is evidence that a substantial house had been built by Sherwood, who had acquired the land in 1851 for $600.

There is also structural evidence that the present building is an addition to an original building, but the house, as it stands, was completed in 1871 by the builder D. Moffat. The interior was noted for its mural decorations, now covered by wallpaper. Like the Menard and Williams-Tucker houses of thirty years earlier, most of the building materials were shipped from Maine; framing and trim were of white pine, the doors of imported mahogany and walnut.

When Mr. Austin died in 1888, the house was inherited by his son Valery. He and his wife, Ida Smith Austin, lived there for more than fifty years. Mrs. Austin died in 1938, after surviving her husband only briefly, and the house was then sold. It is now the property of Mrs. Milo P. Fox.[k]

Congregation B'nai Israel Synagogue, Twenty-second Street between Avenues H and I, 1870

In 1870, the influential and well-received Jewish community of Galveston built the Congregation B'nai Israel Synagogue. Fred Stewart, the architect, had designed a building in the Gothic style with a touch of Moorish Revival.

THE AUSTIN HOUSE, 1868–71.
Henri Cartier-Bresson, Magnum.

THE AUSTIN HOUSE.
Henri Cartier-Bresson, Magnum.

The original center portion was standard Americanized fifteenth-century French Gothic. The west elevation was fitted with thin colonnettes, which supported a rose window of sorts—the finished section looked like an Art Nouveau rose made of tracery, sitting on two stems. The nave openings are more modest, supported by twelfth-century English simple buttresses. Above the openings are the standard brick dentil work so common to the Texas-German brickmason architecture of the era.

In addition to the foiling of the arches, the windows and doors have an upper molding which ends on either side in a volute. In the original building, four giant minarets appeared on the west elevation, confirming this curious mixture of the Moorish and Christian formulas.[1]

B'nai Israel was the center of Jewish life in Galveston, and I. H. Kempner, in *Recalled Recollections*, writes of the year 1879, when his mother's brother,

Joseph Seinsheimer was married to Blanche Fellman—then frequently proclaimed as one of the most beautiful young women in Texas. I had the unique experience of being a "flower girl" with five *girls* to precede the ushers and bridesmaid down the aisle of Temple B'nai Israel at 22nd and Avenue I. My velvet knee-length trousers trimmed with lace elicited much comment. This was decidedly to my embarrassment at the reception which followed the ceremony, but the more lasting when my playmates who had heard about the program, my costume, etc., kept up for weeks continuous sarcastic references to my feminine role.[6]

The original brick of the building was stuccoed in 1890. Nicholas J. Clayton, the great architect of the eighties and nineties in Galveston, was called in and paid $160 as a consultant, and a contractor, Harry Devlin, did the work. In 1900 following the storm, some repairs were made and again Clayton was called in.

In 1953 the building was sold and has now been converted into a Masonic Temple. Successive desecrations have been carried out since that time. The main great west-end tracery windows have been replaced with six aluminum double-hung sash windows; the minarets are gone; and the handsome main entry doors have been removed and replaced with aluminum since Cartier-Bresson's photograph was taken in May 1962.

Notes

1. Andrew Morrison, *The Industries of Galveston* (Galveston: The Metropolitan Publishing Company, 1887), 26, 29.
2. John Maass, *The Gingerbread Age* (New York: Holt, Rinehart and Winston, 1957), 97.
3. *Galveston [Daily] News*, 14 June 1959, 1.
4. Southwick, 8.
5. Morrison, *The Industries of Galveston*, 55.
6. I. H. Kempner, *Recalled Recollections* (privately printed, 1961), 5.

a. The house is now called "Ashton Villa." It is owned by the city and leased to the Galveston Historical Foundation, which operates it as a house museum. The building has undergone major restoration.
b. See chapter 1, note b.
c. Italics added. Author interpolation. Southwick writes, ". . . New Years day."
d. Italics added. Author interpolation. Southwick writes, "center."
e. Italics added. Author interpolation. Southwick uses, "Gen."
f. Italics added. Author interpolation. Southwick writes, ". . . Brown, the general . . ."

CONGREGATION B'NAI ISRAEL SYNAGOGUE, 1870. WEST ELEVATION.
Ezra Stoller.

CONGREGATION B'NAI ISRAEL SYNAGOGUE.
SOUTHWEST CORNER.
Photograph circa 1890.

CONGREGATION B'NAI ISRAEL
SYNAGOGUE. SOUTH ELEVATION.
Henri Cartier-Bresson, Magnum.

g. Italics added. Author interpolation. Southwick writes, "Browns."

h. *Galveston Tri-Weekly News*, 26 October 1858.

i. Beasley notes: "Galveston was a mess in 1865 and for several years thereafter."

j. Of course, since the writing of this book, considerable research has been done on these. All have undergone major renovation.

k. The house now has another owner.

l. According to Whorton and Fox: "It has now been established that the entire western end section was added to the building in 1887 by N. J. Clayton."

CONGREGATION B'NAI ISRAEL
SYNAGOGUE. WEST ELEVATION.
Henri Cartier-Bresson, Magnum.

Earliest Established Professional Architect in the State.

N. J. CLAYTON,

Architect and Superintendent,

OFFICE, 103 EAST STRAND, CORNER 23D STREET.

(Superintendent United States Government Building, Corner Bath Avenue and Church Street.)

GALVESTON REFERENCES:

Sylvain Blum's Residence.
Beach Hotel.
Tremont Hotel.
Harmony Hall.
Artillery Hall.
Masonic Temple.

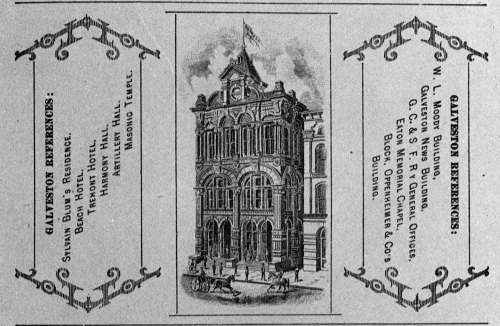

GALVESTON REFERENCES:

W. L. Moody Building.
Galveston News Building.
G. C. & S. F. R'y General Offices.
Eaton Memorial Chapel.
Block, Oppenheimer & Co's
Building.

PLANS, ESTIMATES AND SUPERINTENDENCE FURNISHED FOR EVERY DESCRIPTION OF BUILDING, PUBLIC OR PRIVATE.

STATE REFERENCES:

I. & G. N. R. R. General Offices, Palestine.
Masonic Temple, Palestine.
National Bank, Palestine.
Public School, Ennis.
Van Alstyne Residence, Houston.

CORRESPONDENCE SOLICITED.

P. O. Box 113, Galveston, Texas.

STATE REFERENCES:

Convent, Corsicana.
Ursuline Convent, Dallas.
St. Louis Church, Waco.
Catholic Church, Jeanerette, La.
St. Mary's Church, Austin.

LARGE AND DIFFICULT BUILDING WORK IN BRICK, WOOD, STONE AND IRON.

Fire-Proof Construction, and Modern Residence Designs and Constructions, with Latest Sanitary Appliances and Heating and Ventilating Specialties.

The Clayton Era

In the sixties, the Civil War and the period of recovery after it occupied such a major part of the energy of the people of Galveston that very few buildings were built, and these only during the later years of the decade. Then the Panic of 1873 took its toll, and in the years immediately after it there was almost no building. But by the late seventies, a building boom in Galveston had begun, and Nicholas J. Clayton had become prominent. The eighties and nineties were Clayton's era.

Nicholas J. Clayton, fellow of the American Institute of Architects [AIA], was born on November 1, 1840,[a] in Cork, Ireland. After the death of his father, he was brought to America at the age of two by his mother. In 1864, at twenty-four,[b] he enlisted as a yeoman in the U.S. Navy. After the war, he studied sculpture, architecture and structural engineering with a well-known architect, W. H. Baldwin, in Memphis. He came to Galveston on December 8, 1872, to supervise construction of the new First Presbyterian Church.[c] Clayton's earliest known independent commission in Galveston was the now-demolished Island City Savings Bank of 1874.[d] He was the first professional architect in the state, and this was his first building.[1]

Clayton became a member of the Western Association of Architects in 1885 and automatically became a fellow of the American Institute of Architects under the act of consolidation of the two organizations in 1889. All members of the AIA were fellows after that date, until some years later when the two grades of membership were reestablished.[2]

Clayton apparently was a very shy man. Little is written of him in the chronicles of the era; he does not appear in the "mug" books of Galveston and other cities of the West, so popular in the nineties. During his bachelor days in Galveston, he spent a great deal of time with the children of St. Mary's Orphanage, bringing them presents regularly and personally conducting the fireworks display on New Year's Eve and other holidays.

When he was close to fifty, he married Miss Mary Ducie, twenty years his junior, whose father, what we now might call an artist-decorator, had executed the interiors of Clayton's most splendid work, the Gresham House. The Claytons had five children.

When he died on December 9, 1916, the *Galveston [Daily] News* carried the briefest type of death notice in the obituary column—no editorials, no stock-taking of the tremendous contribution of this talented man.

The architecture of Galveston from 1873 until 1900 was so dominated by Clayton that this chapter is properly entitled The Clayton Era.

The Block-Oppenheimer Building, 2314 Strand, 1881–82[e]

Nicholas J. Clayton, Architect

Block-Oppenheimer is not really very different in plan from the undefined commercial blocks of the sixties and seventies commonly found in most American cities. It represents, however, a transitional stage between the commercial blocks of the south side of the Strand and the specialized build-

ings that were to come later. The buildings of the sixties and seventies were constructed for the needs of any kind of business, with three or four identical upper stories which could be subdivided into offices or storerooms.

Specialization in the commercial block was at first shown on the exterior, by variety in window spacing and details. Instead of the absolutely regular bay spacing seen in the Salvation Army Building and Henry's Bookstore, the Block-Oppenheimer four-story façade is broken into a large central bay made up of three smaller elements, plus a wider bay on each side. The window sizes change with each floor; the upper story has the beginnings of a strong Romanesque feeling. The cornice, which was destroyed in the 1900 storm, was one of the great elaborations of the time and signified that this was a building which had been designed by an architect for a special client for his special use, in this case, a wholesale dealer and importer of dry goods, shoes, hats and notions. The cornice had four giant corbels supporting elaborate pedestals above the cornice line, cast-iron balustrades and the name of the building set some sixty feet above eye level, framed in scrolls and topped with a winged abstract bird, further topped by the national ensign.

The ground floor was originally set four feet above the level of the street so that dray wagons could back up to the service entrances. It is now at street level as a result of the grade raising of 1903–5.[f]

Clayton continued the somewhat questionable practice of using cast iron on the ground floor, except that in this building the cast iron is anything but the tinlike facing of the commercial blocks across the street. Clayton's use of the material consists of structural columns supporting the entire face of the four-story structure above. The columns are semidetached from the structure with a decorated, pierced web between the inner and outer columns which bespeaks knowledge of the use of the material.

Clayton was not guilty of what [A. W. N.] Pugin described as the increasing confusion of ornament with design: "It is impossible to enumerate half the absurdities of modern metal-workers; but all these proceed from the false notion of *disguising* instead of *beautifying* articles of utility."[g] These columns are beautified articles of utility. The ironwork was cast in Galveston at the Walsh and Cleary Iron Foundry, also known as the Galveston Iron Works. Walsh and Cleary were early settlers and were responsible for much of the ironwork in Galveston. The firm did most of the work for the railroads and steamships and was responsible for the castings necessary for most of the manufacturing activity of the town.

The Block-Oppenheimer Building has been occupied for many years by the firm of Flood and Calvert.[h]

St. Mary's Infirmary, 701 Market Street, 1874 (Demolished 1965)[i]

Nicholas J. Clayton, Architect

Nicholas Clayton was an ardent Catholic. It is therefore understandable that one of his first large commissions was St. Mary's Infirmary in 1874. St. Mary's, an institution which had been established in 1866, was under the supervision of the Sisters of Charity of the Incarnate Word. St. Mary's is the oldest hospital in Texas, is still in being [*sic*], and portions of the original building are still standing.

THE BLOCK-OPPENHEIMER
BUILDING, 1881–82.
NICHOLAS J. CLAYTON, ARCHITECT.
DETAIL AT ENTRY.
Henri Cartier-Bresson, Magnum.

St. Mary's Infirmary, 1874.
Nicholas J. Clayton, architect.
Ezra Stoller.

St. Mary's Infirmary.
Photograph circa 1890.

The Voelcker House, 1811 Avenue E, 1887

(Demolished)ʲ

The Voelcker House with the elaborate cross-beaming of its tower is a fair example of the "stick style" which is duplicated on the bay windows of the east end, not shown in the photographs. By the 1860s the use of medieval half-timber was not uncommon, a symptom of the renewed interest in wood for its own sake. The asymmetric plan indicates the desire of the seventies for picturesque variety. The two-story porch extending around the corner on the north elevation is in the true Galveston style and is a feature of every Galveston house whatever its architectural style. Thus, in the evening the occupants could escape the heat built up in the house during the day. The fact that the building faces north, away from the prevailing breeze, made little difference. The style, once established, became a thing in itself.

Professor Voelcker was associated with the J. J. Schott Manufacturing Company. This enterprising organization in 1886 was a huge drug business which originated the famous Moxie Nerve Food. Moxie syrup was to become by the 1920s a national soda drink. The popularity of Moxie made J. J. Schott one of Galveston's major manufacturers.

The building remained in the Voelcker family until 1915 when it was sold to Robert E. Moreland. In 1941 it was owned briefly by Dorothy Helen Adoue. It was owned by Thomas F. Davis from 1941 to 1956, when it was bought by Ella Mae Starnes, the present owner.

The Sawyer-Flood House, 1528 Broadway, circa 1879

(Demolished 1965)ᵏ

On Broadway, at the corner of Sixteenth Street, stood the saddest of all the great Galveston palaces. This wood mansion, probably built about 1879, and at the time of its demolition inhabited by Negro squatters, is typical of the prosperous American house of that decade. Little distinguished it from the great Victorian mansions of the eastern United States except the high stuccoed brick base, a feature of all Galveston houses, built to protect them from high water. The plan, bay windows, gable ends, cupola, brackets and two-tiered porch were all in the standard upper middle-class carpenter vernacular. The porch, facing the southwest rather than the prevailing breeze of the southeast, was a further clue that a stock plan from the builder's handbook was the inspiration.

At first glance it was apparent that the Sawyer-Flood House, probably quite by accident, was ideally suited to the subtropical heat of Galveston. The large floor-to-ceiling windows admitted light by day and air by night, but the high, central tower with its windows was most admirably adapted as a ventilator, rising above the roof of the house. The open tower windows could trap any breeze that might come their way at the same time as they expelled the rising heat. We speak so much of functionality today that the word no longer has any meaning. Here, in this house, the architecture bore such a perfect relation to the climate that the word is valid.

At the time it was built there was not complete agreement as to the design of houses such as the Sawyer-Flood House. Alexander Downing, who was responsible for many of the copybooks which spread throughout the U.S. in the fifties, sixties and seventies and quoted in Gloag, *Victorian Taste*, wrote:

There is a glaring want of truthfulness sometimes practised in this country by ignorant builders, that deserves condemnation at all times. This is seen in the attempt to express a style of architecture, which demands massiveness, weight and solidity, in a material that possesses none of these qualities. We could point to two or three of these imitations of Gothic castles, with towers and battlements built of wood. Nothing can well be more paltry and contemptible. The sugar castles of confectioners and pastrycooks are far more admirable as works of art. If a man is ambitious of attracting attention by his house, and can only afford wood, let him (if he can content himself with nothing appropriate) build a gigantic wigwam of logs and bark, even a shingle palace, but not attempt mock battlements of pine boards, and strong towers of thin plank. The imposition attempted, is more than even the most uneducated person of native sense can possibly bear.[l]

There is considerable doubt as to who actually built the house. The first records at the Stewart Title Company in Galveston indicate that J. H. Shropshire owned the site from 1867 through 1873. James Huffmaster owned it from 1873 through 1879, and there is a possibility that he was the builder. However, it is more likely that Captain Jeremiah N. Sawyer, who purchased the site in 1879, built the house in that year. Owing to the long occupancy of the house by two families, Captain Sawyer, from 1879 through 1905, and the E. O. Flood family, from 1905 to 1943, the house was known as the Sawyer-Flood House.

Flood was born in New York and came to Galveston in 1876. When he bought the house in 1905, he had for at least fifteen years been the most important coal dealer in Galveston. Strangely enough, in that same year, 1905, oil was discovered at Spindletop, making the use of coal as a source of energy such an oddity that children on the Gulf Coast today are shown pieces of coal as a rare mineral. Flood was engaged in both the wholesale and the retail market for coal in Galveston. He supplied fuel for steamships and purchased coal in great quantities direct from Pennsylvania, bringing it in steamship loads. Flood also owned a small shipping firm. He operated a steamship, the *Manteo*, which ran between Galveston and New Orleans and Galveston and Brownsville, and was credited with helping to build up the lower Rio Grande and Brownsville area by keeping the rail rates on freight at par with his more reasonable water rates.

Flood maintained a downtown office at 2115 Mechanic Street and another office at the coalyard located in the port at Avenue A and Eighteenth Street, where he had extensive facilities at Pier 20.

George D. Flood owned the house from 1943 to 1948, during which time it was leased to the Home Finance Agency for wartime housing. It has been owned by the Druss Real Estate Company since 1948.

The Galveston Pavilion, Twenty-first Street and Avenue Q, 1881

(Burned 1883)[m]

Nicholas J. Clayton, Architect

The Galveston City Railway Company in 1880 decided to increase their patronage by building a giant pavilion on the beach at Twenty-first Street and Avenue Q. The beach had long been used for bathing, but this was the first specifically resort-type structure built. All prior building on the beach had been either mercantile or residential. In his book *The Industries of Galveston*, Andrew

Morrison wrote:

Galveston has, in truth both favor and patronage. As nature made it, the beach lying within the city limits, is acknowledged one of the finest drives and bathing places in the world. During the summer months, the sea breeze, blowing from the balmy bosom of the gulf reduces the heat to a most refreshing temperature. The pavilion and other places of resort, to which the street cars ran for years back, brought from the interior and from distant points as well, summer visitors.[3]

The Galveston Pavilion was more influenced by the work and teaching of Alexander Downing than any other building in Clayton's career. Downing's "cottage style" of the thirties and forties had been a violent reaction to the Greek Revival of the era. During the fifties, Italianate villas such as the J. M. Brown House represented an equally violent reaction to the cottage style. There then developed in the sixties the Second Empire mansarded buildings in masonry and wood, such as St. Mary's Infirmary.

By the early seventies, however, this reaction toward the heavy and the sculptural had in general run its course, and the "stick style," the name coined by the brilliant young architectural historian Vincent Scully, was after 1875 the major expression of American wood vernacular architecture inspired by Alexander Downing's cottage style.

The Galveston Pavilion was an excellent example in which the diagonal sticks took over the architectural fabric. It was what might be called a baroque manipulation of the stick style. Another

such structure, the New Jersey State Building, designed five years earlier by Carl Pfeiffer for the Philadelphia Centennial of 1876, was a high point of skeletal expression — all stick and no wall. Clayton's Pavilion was to go further. In his building the sticks were no longer sufficient. Accordingly he inserted four huge steel arches to carry the load on which the wood trusses rested. Perhaps in no other building was the stick style carried to the point where it was insufficient as a basic structural system. Clayton took the esthetic of the cottage and blew it up to a heroic scale for which the building methods of the cottage were totally inadequate. Freedom to experiment was an essential of the style. This freedom was the legacy of mid-century America to the architectural development which was to follow. Clayton only touched the style occasionally, but when he did, it was in the grand manner.

Clayton shared credit for the pavilion with an engineer, for the drawings were marked Clayton & Lynch. This was the first building in Galveston to have electric lights (1882), and [it] was built by contractor Harry Devlin. The building survived only two years. It burned to the ground in twenty-five minutes in a fire which began at 2:00 A.M. on August 1, 1883.

Harmony Hall, Church and Twenty-second streets, 1881

(Burned 1928)[n]

Nicholas J. Clayton, Architect

There is an apocryphal story told of Sir Christopher Wren, the architect of St. Paul's Cathedral in London. According to this, Wren so loved his creation that near the end of his life he bought a little house directly opposite, so that each morning he might view it afresh. Harmony Hall may have held the same place in the heart of Nicholas Clayton. His earlier works, Block-Oppenheimer and St. Mary's Infirmary,[o] were minor and tentative compared to the triumphant

baroque violence of Harmony Hall.

The elaborate cornice on Block-Oppenheimer is simplicity itself compared to the extravagances of Harmony Hall. Here, the cornices are not mere additions but an integral part of the scheme. The pedestals, the broken pediments, the bullnose windows, the broken entablatures, the endless delight of Renaissance vocabulary — all are here a unified whole which would have been a notable building even in the Paris of the era. In fact, there is little question that Garnier's opera house in Paris had strong influence. There is still the remnant of American Victorian in the windows and the classical pediments of the cornices, but this is a great Neo-Renaissance building.

The interior was as elaborate as the exterior. French and Italian Renaissance decor was everywhere. The forty-foot clear span in the auditorium was trussed with heavy wood bents; the balcony hung from the upper roof trusses with two-inch cast-iron tension rods. The cost was well over $80,000; Harry Devlin was the contractor.

The Harmony Club was organized in the 1870s by a group of prominent Jewish citizens of Galveston for social and business purposes. By 1881, the Harmony Hall Association, of which Albert Weis was president and J. Seinsheimer secretary, were in a position to realize their ambitions.

Here were held all the elaborate functions of Jewish social life. While membership was limited in the beginning to Jews, the Harmony Hall Association was later organized as the Union Club. Not only were the large balls of the city held in the building, but all Sunday school entertainments and the annual Purim balls of Congregation B'nai Israel were held there.[4]

In the late nineties, the club was in financial difficulties, and Harmony Hall was rented to the Galveston Business University. Shortly thereafter John Sealy acquired the property. The 1900 storm severely damaged the building. Portions of the roof and much of the cornice were blown away. Rapid growth of the Galveston Scottish Rite bodies immediately after 1900 brought about a need for larger quarters, and since Harmony Hall in its damaged condition was on the market, it was purchased by them on January 27, 1902.[5]

Harmony Hall was destroyed by fire on February 5, 1928.

The Stewart Title Building, 230 Twenty-second Street, 1882

Eugene T. Heiner, Architect[p]

The biggest and most important merchants in Galveston in the eighties were Kauffman & Runge—importers of coffee and liquors, grocers, factors and commission merchants—located at the corner of Mechanic and Twenty-second streets.

In any description of this house the facts themselves are sufficient to indicate, without exaggeration, that it is one of uncommon resources and noteworthy characteristics. It is an old house, and a strong house, and a house, in its methods and management, fully up to the best standard prevailing in the other large cities of the country.[q]

The grocery trade of the company was principally with patrons in Texas. But cotton shipments were made to Mexico, England, France, Germany, Russia and, in fact, to almost all parts of the world.

One steamer alone, since the firm were agents for the

North German Lloyd, whose port of destination was changed in 1878 from New Orleans to Galveston, brought here from Bremen over 1000 German immigrants, a people who proved to be a most valuable accession to the rural population of Texas.[6]

Mr. Kauffman had established the company in 1842. In 1872, the firm name became Kauffman & Runge. Kauffman, a native of Galveston, was brought up to the business; he was the Austrian consul of the port, and Runge was consul of the newly established German Empire. Runge had been an alderman of the city and was then city treasurer. He served two terms on the Board of Aldermen of Galveston, between the years 1877

THE VOELCKER RESIDENCE, 1887.
DETAIL OF NORTH ELEVATION.
Henri Cartier-Bresson, Magnum.

RESIDENCE OF PROF. R. VOELCKER (J. J. SCHOTT—"MOXIE"—M'F'G CO.)

THE VOELCKER RESIDENCE.
Engraving from Andrew Morrison's
Industries of Galveston, *published*
1887.

RIGHT: THE VOELCKER RESIDENCE.
Henri Cartier-Bresson, Magnum.

THE SAWYER-FLOOD HOUSE.
DETAIL OF BAY WINDOW AT FRONT
ENTRY.
Henri Cartier-Bresson, Magnum.

LEFT: THE SAWYER-FLOOD HOUSE,
CIRCA 1879.
Henri Cartier-Bresson, Magnum

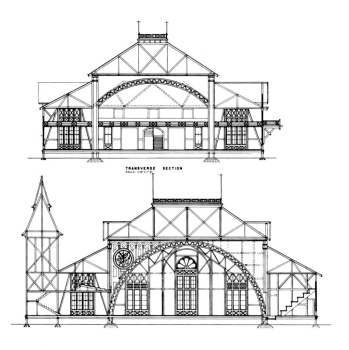

THE GALVESTON PAVILION, 1881.
HISTORIC AMERICAN BUILDINGS
SURVEY, UNDER THE DIRECTION OF
THE U.S. DEPARTMENT OF THE
INTERIOR, NATIONAL PARKS
SERVICE BRANCH OF PLANS AND
DESIGN, 1935.

THE GALVESTON PAVILION
(BURNED 1883).
NICHOLAS J. CLAYTON, ARCHITECT.
Photograph circa 1882.

HARMONY HALL, 1881.
NICHOLAS J. CLAYTON, ARCHITECT.
Photograph circa 1890.

LEFT: THE STEWART TITLE
BUILDING (ORIGINALLY KAUFFMAN
& RUNGE), 1882.
EUGENE T. HEINER, ARCHITECT.
DETAIL OF WEST ELEVATION.
Henri Cartier-Bresson, Magnum.

THE KAUFFMAN & RUNGE BUILDING
(PRESENTLY THE STEWART TITLE
BUILDING).
Photograph circa 1890.

[99]

RIGHT TO LEFT, THE STEWART
TITLE BUILDING, NEXT THE
TRUEHEART-ADRIANCE
BUILDING, AND CENTER, THE
FIRST NATIONAL BANK
BUILDING, CIRCA 1878.
DESIGN ATTRIBUTED TO J. M.
BROWN, WHO IS ALSO SAID
TO HAVE SUPERVISED ITS
CONSTRUCTION.
Henri Cartier-Bresson, Magnum.

and 1880, and while chairman of the Finance Committee brought the municipality into sound financial condition by reducing the rate of interest on bonded indebtedness from 10 and 12 percent to 5 and 8 percent. His investments in interests outside his partnership in the house were various and widespread. He was president of the First National Bank and of the Texas Land and Loan Company; vice president of the Southern Cotton Press Company; a director of the Texas Cotton Press Company and of the Galveston City Railway. He was identified by property as well as [by] social ties with the best interests of the city.

Kauffman & Runge occupied a business block covering 85 by 120 feet, constructed of Philadelphia pressed brick. The building was sold to Maco Stewart, Sr., in 1905, who transferred title to the Security Building Company. Ever since, it has been the home of the Stewart Title Company, the first title company in Texas.

Known as "the Kremlin" today, it is painted red except for the white keystones in the center of the arches and has a vigorous—almost brutal—aspect due to the elegant cornice's being blown off in the storm of 1900.[r] Like the unspecialized blocks of earlier years, this four-story business palace is a straightforward masonry wall-bearing structure, standard for the time in all its aspects, with interior cast-iron supporting columns. It represents typical work done during Galveston's busiest era[s] and almost seems to be something rushed through to completion. There is nowhere evidence of the care Clayton[t] showered on the small, next-door Trueheart-Adriance Building of the year before. This one was straight business, and it has served that purpose for eighty years.

The H. M. Trueheart-Adriance Building, 212 Twenty-second Street, 1882

Nicholas J. Clayton, Architect

By 1882 Clayton was firmly established and was commissioned to do an urbane, small business building for H. M. Trueheart, whose firm had the distinction of being the oldest real estate firm in Texas. Almost as well known as the firm itself was the little iron Negro boy installed for hitching post purposes in the days of the horse and carriage, which stood at the old post for seventy-five years to taunt antique hunters.

The firm was first organized by A. F. James in January 1857. Soon thereafter, it was acquired by H. M. Trueheart, pioneer Galveston businessman. In 1872 John Adriance joined the firm as a partner, and in 1884 Lucian Minor, who lost his life in the 1900 storm, was admitted. On the death of Mr. Trueheart, the firm name was changed to John Adriance & Sons.

The firm was composed in the 1930s of H. T. Adriance, C. D. Adriance and John Adriance, Jr., sons of John Adriance. The law firm of James B. and Charles J. Stubbs occupied the second floor of the building for almost three-quarters of a century.

The clientele of the firm, officials declared, extended throughout the United States and Europe. One client resided in Egypt. The firm operated for about a hundred years. It was the second oldest active depositor of the Hutchings-Sealy National Bank, successors to Ball, Hutchings & Company. V. L. Baulard & Company, successors to Rice & Baulard, was the first and oldest active depositor.[7]

Like so much Victorian architecture, the building is an almost incredible mixture of architectural motifs. On the ground floor are decorative cast-iron semidetached columns, two of which seem to support elaborate brick pilaster columns above. The ogee curves of the upper sash on the ground

THE TRUEHEART-ADRIANCE BUILDING, 1882.

DETAIL OF WEST ELEVATION.

Henri Cartier-Bresson, Magnum.

THE TRUEHEART-ADRIANCE
BUILDING.
Present-day ink drawing.

RIGHT: THE TRUEHEART-ADRIANCE
BUILDING (TO THE RIGHT, LOOKING
NORTH).
Ezra Stoller.

floor show the flourish of Clayton at his best.

The second floor is close to a true *piano nobile* with handsome floor-to-ceiling windows. The brickwork detailing on both the first and second floors is a delightful study of raised paneling. The paneled pilasters are capped with flat Corinthian capitals which look almost Mayan or Aztec.

The third floor has an arcade of narrow brick Romanesque windows, which are a prototype of the windows of the Romanesque buildings Clayton was to design in the next decade. The building is topped with a Victorian Greek cornice complete with dentils and antefixes and a small center pediment. Whether this undeniably conscious effort at Greek detailing was a forerunner of the Neo-Renaissance Revival which followed the Chicago World's Fair of 1893 or whether it was a harking back to the days of Greek Revival forty years before is difficult to say.

The whole elevation, though covered with applied decor from a thousand years of varied architectural sources, undeniably holds together. It precedes the W. L. Moody Building by a year and is, in a sense, an earlier version of it.[u]

The J. E. Wallis House, 1502 Avenue I, 1882

(Demolished 1962)[v]

J. E. Wallis and his brother, J. C. Wallis, set up one of the pioneer grocery firms of Galveston. They had established a general merchandising business in Washington County prior to the Civil War and had there been involved in cotton factoring. In 1865 they moved to Galveston and joined with A. J. Landes to form the firm Wallis, Landes and Company, "taking into consideration the extent of its varied transactions, its spirited management and liberal methods, to be rated with the most substantial firms not of Galveston alone, but of the South."[8]

The Wallis House differs little from the standard large merchant house anywhere in the country in the decade of the eighties, except for the cast-iron porches with their almost Art Nouveau detailing. The double-tiered porches were oriented to the south and east to catch the prevailing breeze. The windows, like the ceilings, are enormously high to make the house habitable in the subtropic climate.

The house had a full-story basement prior to the grade raising of 1903–5.[w] The swallowing up of this ground story at that time took much away from the house. The main story with its extremely high ceilings, plus the attic set on a full story, must have been an imposing sight. The small tower above roof level would have then been the fifth floor.

[The] design for the roof . . . was in transition from the high dormers of the mansard and the flatter pitches of the Neo-Renaissance. The entire building was transitional. It is half American Victorian and half Renaissance.

The house remained in the Wallis family until 1913. There was then a fairly rapid succession of owners: Frances E. Kelly (1913–18), Herbert A. Wood (1918–19), George Hagelstein (1919), E. E. Whitaker (1919–20), P. J. Bellow (1920–21), Ruby D. Smith (1923–53) and Mrs. George A. Davis (1953–62). Mrs. Davis ordered the building razed in May 1962 on the grounds that it was too expensive to maintain. Happily, Cartier-Bresson was in Galveston as the demolition crew arrived.

I. H. Kempner, in his *Recalled Recollections*, speaks of his parents' home (now demolished) at Twentieth Street and Avenue M. The house was of the same era as the Wallis House, and life must have been much the same in both:

THE J. E. WALLIS RESIDENCE, 1882 (DEMOLISHED 1962).
Henri Cartier-Bresson, Magnum.

THE J. E. WALLIS
RESIDENCE.
Henri Cartier-Bresson, Magnum.

LEFT AND RIGHT, THE J. E.
WALLIS RESIDENCE.
Henri Cartier-Bresson, Magnum.

. . . a large and wooden structure facing north, with a long hall, probably fifty feet [in] length, about ten feet wide, down the center, and a large sitting room and dining room on the right as one entered. The house faced north. There was a wide porch downstairs only, its length the width of the house, approximately fifty feet long. On the left as one entered were a parlor and dining room, on the right a sitting room and library. The sitting room and dining room, enjoying southern exposure and our vaunted gulf breezes, were by far more frequently used. Almost all the rooms were about eighteen by twenty feet or larger. I do not recall at all well the upstairs arrangement except the emphasis on southern exposure accorded to two rooms on each side of the hall.

A porch on the south of the main house, both upstairs and down, corresponded to the one on the north. The downstairs southern porch led off to a separate lattice enclosed terrace structure of kitchen, pantry, wine storage space and groceries which were brought in large containers. Father bought coffee by 300 pound bags (Mocha and Java) from Mexico; rice ordered in barrels from South Carolina, wine from France by the cask. Living quarters were provided on the premises for the cook, several maids, coachman and butler.[x]

The W. L. Moody Building, Strand and Twenty-second Street, 1883

Nicholas J. Clayton, Architect

Of all the early financial giants of Texas, Colonel W. L. Moody ranked first. The empire which the Colonel founded still exists. Only a few years ago the fortune was estimated at $500 million, and the W. L. Moody Charitable Trust of Galveston is said to be worth $400 million.

Andrew Morrison, in *The Industries of Galveston*, gives a brief but vivid biography of the titan. Colonel Moody came to Freestone County, Texas, in 1852, from Virginia, where he had been educated at the University of Virginia. He had been colonel of a Texas regiment of the Confederate forces, had been severely wounded in Jackson, Mississippi, and had been in command of the Confederate post at Austin at the end of the war.

In 1865 he came to Galveston as a cotton factor and soon became prominent as one of the largest dealers in the market. At first he had partners. The firm was known as Moody, Bradley and Company, then Moody and Jemison. In 1881 the firm of W. L. Moody and Company was established, which included his own vast interests and those of his brother L. F. Moody. His oldest son, W. L. Moody, Jr., was born in Galveston, bred to the business and came back to work for his father after a liberal education in Europe.[9] He became a junior partner on his twenty-first birthday, January 25, 1886. In 1881, Colonel Moody was made president of the Cotton Exchange. About the same time, he was a member of the legislature and was appointed by Governor Coke as financial agent for the sale of almost $2 million in state bonds, "a preferment that was in itself an indication of his capacity for affairs."[10]

In 1883 the corner of Twenty-second and Strand streets was the hub of Galveston's financial interests, with banks occupying strategic locations within the immediate area. Nicholas Clayton, who had now been in Galveston for nine years, was hired to build this business palace—the seat of empire. The ground cost $20,000, the building, $40,000.

W. L. Moody, Jr., in the September 1933 *House of Moody Magazine*, wrote:[y]

The building was originally built by Col. Moody and his partner, Col. E. S. Jemison, but in the dissolution of their partnership, Col. Moody got the building as his share.

"I was off at school when the building was erected,"

THE W. L. MOODY BUILDING, 1883.
NICHOLAS J. CLAYTON, ARCHITECT.
Ezra Stoller.

THE W. L. MOODY BUILDING.
Photograph circa 1890.

THE W. L. MOODY BUILDING.
Ezra Stoller.

[Mr. W. L. Moody, Jr., said.] "My father and Colonel Jemison owned a brickyard at Morgan's Point, and the bricks used in the building were made at that place. The rear part of the building was laid in salt water, and I asked my father how they built it in the water, and he explained that they put the bricks together on a plant, cemented them together, and then sank the whole thing in the water. We used to be able to catch fish from the rear windows of the building."[z]

The building as originally built was four stories high. Clayton applied to the front gigantic semide-tached four-story pillars with heavy rustication on the lower floors and mildly Pompeian detailing in the upper floors. The cornice was the usual magnificent affair with garlanded corbels, Greek pediments and elegant clocks topping each semidetached column. A Palladian motif appeared on the fourth floor of the east elevation, suggesting the Renaissance Revival that was to come in the nineties.

The Moody Building owes much to the Trueheart-Adriance Building, built the year before, in 1882. In that one year one can see the transition from romantic or Victorian to Neo-Renaissance.

On the ground floor are peculiarly bizarre and jagged cast-iron columns, a carry-over in concept from the sixties and seventies. These cast-iron columns are practically all that is left of the original architectural expression.

Although the building was first built to house the Moody-Jemison cotton business, it was for a number of years the headquarters of the Galveston Cotton Exchange, which Colonel Moody was instrumental in organizing. The C. M. Pearre wholesale grocery firm—one of the larger business establishments in the old days—occupied the first floor. Colonel Moody bought Moritz Kopperl's interest in the National Bank of Texas, the third oldest national bank in Texas and then moved the bank over into the corner of the building. This bank occupied the corner for several years. Meanwhile, the W. L. Moody Bank was organized, and it occupied quarters next door to the National Bank of Texas. Ultimately, the Moody Bank absorbed the National Bank of Texas, and occupied the entire part of the first floor facing Strand, while the cotton business occupied the part facing Twenty-second Street.[a†]

About two months before the storm, the top floor was leased to the George H. McFadden cotton firm. They built a big skylight in the roof, and the hurricane broke in the skylight and cut off the entire top story of the building. Instead of rebuilding this story on to the building, a roof was put on and the height of the building reduced to three stories. The first people that went to work here after the storm were the men I put to work to clear away the debris on Strand so that we could open the bank. The storm was on a Saturday night. We had to get all the debris cleared away on Sunday so that the bank could be opened on Monday. For a long number of years, the bank and the cotton firm occupied their quarters in the building. Then, when the American National Insurance Company was first organized, this building was its original home. The Insurance Company occupied the third floor of the building, until its business had so expanded that more extensive quarters were needed.[11]

When he died in 1954, W. L. Moody, Jr., was reputed to be among the ten richest men in the United States. His holdings reached far beyond the confines of Galveston. The Moody-owned American National Life Insurance Company is one of the twenty largest in the nation, with policies worth at least $2.5 billion. The Affiliated National Hotels include hotels in Washington, D. C., Indianapolis, Omaha, Norfolk, Birmingham, Mobile, New Orleans, Dallas and eight other Texas cities, in addition to the Galvez, the Jean Lafitte and two others in Galveston.

The Moody interests, until recently, included both Galveston newspapers, the morning *News* and the afternoon *Tribune*. There is almost nothing in the city of a profitable nature in which the family has not been interested, except oil.

Notably abstemious in their personal habits, the Moodys for years watched Galveston make a name for itself as a town devoted to the pursuit of pleasure.

Under the benign eye of the late Sam Maceo, polite drinking, dining, and gambling flourished openly in the luxurious Balinese Room, on a private pier out over the beach. These diversions, including sex, could also be found in a variety of less elegant places around the city. Since Maceo's death, all but the more discreet forms of amusement have been banished. Much of the gambling has moved into new quarters at resorts down the coast.[12]

The Beach Hotel, Corner of Tremont and the Beach, 1883 (Burned 1898)

Nicholas J. Clayton, Architect

Built two years after Harmony Hall and the Galveston Pavilion, the Beach Hotel represents, in some ways, a retrogression for Clayton. The Beach Hotel harks back to the great hotels of the seventies, displaying a mansard tower and the stick style at its most splendid. Unquestionably it was influenced by the San Francisco Palace, with its glass roof and grand court, which did not survive the great earthquake and fire. Perhaps, however, the Beach Hotel was most influenced by two showplaces of Saratoga Springs, the United States Hotel and the Grand Union. Clayton's last mansard had been St. Mary's Infirmary of 1874. In the central tower and roof of the Beach Hotel, he revived the style which had gone out of fashion almost ten years before. The *Galveston [Daily] News* of July 3, 1883,[b†] commented: "The architect evidently had in mind the commodious and picturesque buildings of the reign of Queen Anne, making a happy combination of the pointed and curved arches of the gothic with the more substantial works of ancient and modern times."[c†]

The plan of the three-storied, three-pavilioned building lent itself admirably to the advantages of the location—the view and the sea breezes. Most rooms were corner rooms. Large windows ran from floor to ceiling, and an American Gothic two-story porch shaded the lower stories and provided terraces for rockers. The building was described as "three pavilions,"[d†] octagonal in shape, forming three sides of a rectangular figure broken in the center by the main or central pavilion projection. Thus, by connecting these pavilions, the result was a figure similar to the letter "E." All of these pavilion promenades were surrounded by openwork balustrades.

As in the Galveston Pavilion, Clayton let himself go in a blaze of color; this applied particularly to the roof. This was painted in giant Siennese stripes of red and white, the earlier more permanent "constructive coloration"[e†] of contrasting marble. Color on the beach was not only advocated but put into practice by the Galvestonians of the eighties, "for the appearance of the hotel was nothing if not gay and attractive."[f†] The structure itself, ornate with grillwork and numerous gables, was painted a delicate mauve, the eaves, a golden green. A triumph of the architect's art was the dome, which was painted such a variety of colors as to be almost dazzling. The ridges of the roof of the east and west pavilions, surmounted by iron cresting of bronze and gold with terminal pieces, completed the finish, and the whole was crowned with the octagonal dome, rising 125 feet above the ground from the main or central pavilion. From the apex of the dome a flagstaff extended, capped by a weather vane.

To make the building stable, it was set on three hundred piles driven deep into the sand. These piles were put together in clusters to form the massive supports and became an integral part of the building, "enabling it to resist the severest shocks it could be subjected to."[g†]

For its time the hotel was enormous. Its three stories and basement contained two hundred available rooms. It was 245 feet in length, with verandas 18 feet in width, extending around the front and sides, and it was 112 feet in depth.

The inside of the building was "artistically and comfortably" furnished and decorated. Much of the wainscot-

The Beach Hotel, 1883.
Nicholas J. Clayton, architect.
Photograph circa 1890.

THE BEACH HOTEL.
NICHOLAS J. CLAYTON,
ARCHITECT.
Photograph circa 1890.

ing was made of cypress and curled pine *from Beaumont, Texas and from the lobby to the kitchen "no detail was omitted" that might add attractiveness or comfort. The kitchen was a two-story building detached from the hotel, this in order to lessen the possibility of fires.*[h†] Against these, the most elaborate precautions were taken. Hoses were placed at short intervals along the corridors; stair-cases were widely separated and watchmen patrolled the building night and day.[13]

The hotel sat right on the sand. No barrier of swimming pools, gardens, seawalls separated the guest from the beach and the water; there was only a streetcar line, which deposited the vacationer at either of the two great seaside stairways.

A grand celebration marked the opening on July 3, 1883. The magnificent new structure was "beautifully illuminated with 30 Brush electric lights while sweet sounds from Professor Boos' Brass Band were wafted out in the gentle gulf breeze."[i†] J. Harvey Pierce, first manager of the hostelry, conducted his guests on an inspection tour while Mrs. Pierce showed the ladies the intricacies of the kitchen and linen closets. The Otis hydraulic elevator was admired and tried, and the various other features drew much comment. Later, over many bottles of champagne, toasts to the success of the Beach Hotel were drunk, and revelry continued until a late hour. Guests were received on July 4, and all of the "migratory birds of fashion"[i†] were attracted to its hospitality.

During the years from 1883 to 1898 the Beach Hotel entertained many distinguished guests, among them President Benjamin Harrison and Postmaster General John Wanamaker. It was one of the outstanding features of the city and was famous all over the United States.

Week ends then had not been adopted from English custom, the hotel became a mecca of those Texans who first indulged in the luxury of vacations and extracurricular matrimonial escapades. Its wide porches on four stories were the rendezvous of moonlight strolls of couples hastening to the darker area of the porches and gave great opportunities to the watchdog dowagers of the period to expand the range and explore the tendencies of the subjects of their gossip. They would particularly shoot their suspicions at the targets of brash visiting younger females who, sought by the gay blades of the day, would force the dowagers to sit up as late as eleven o'clock; this gossip contingent hoping to peek in the more retired and casual corners of the porches and find more fuel for next day's conversation. Other good women of the period would sit around the lobby and speculate, as each couple registered, whether they were really husband and wife.[14]

Plans for a beach hotel had been first proposed by Colonel W. H. Sinclair, president of the Galveston City Railroad Company, in the summer of 1882, but the idea met with a singular lack of enthusiasm, in spite of the fact that the sum to be expended was set at only $50,000. Later, when Colonel Sinclair announced that the project was to be given up and lumber already purchased sold at auction, a group of public-spirited citizens met and decided to help finance the hotel. When all the arrangements were completed, finances were obtained from the originator of the plan, from railroads running into Galveston and from private citizens by means of public-indebtedness bonds. A truly first-class resort hotel was decided upon, to cost the then exorbitant sum of $100,000. Property extending from what was then Tremont Street and Avenue R to Twenty-first Street was purchased, and work on the structure went steadily forward.[15]

The building actually cost over $260,000 to build. The rush to get it finished in time for the summer season of 1883 was so great that construction went on at night under electric lights. The City Railroad Company had backed the Beach Hotel as heavily as it had the Galveston Pavilion, but the hotel consistently lost money and was finally sold by the sheriff for taxes. It burned to the ground early in the morning of July 23, 1898.

The origin of the fire was mysterious—another fire had started in the same place in the boiler room several weeks before—but the cause could only be guessed. Nothing remained but the circular brick smokestack. Entirely of wood, the huge building made a splendid spectacle as it burned,

THE GALVESTON NEWS BUILDING.
Ezra Stoller.

THE GALVESTON NEWS BUILDING,
1883–84. NICHOLAS J. CLAYTON,
ARCHITECT.
Ezra Stoller.

LEFT: THE GALVESTON NEWS
BUILDING. DETAIL AT ENTRY.
Ezra Stoller.

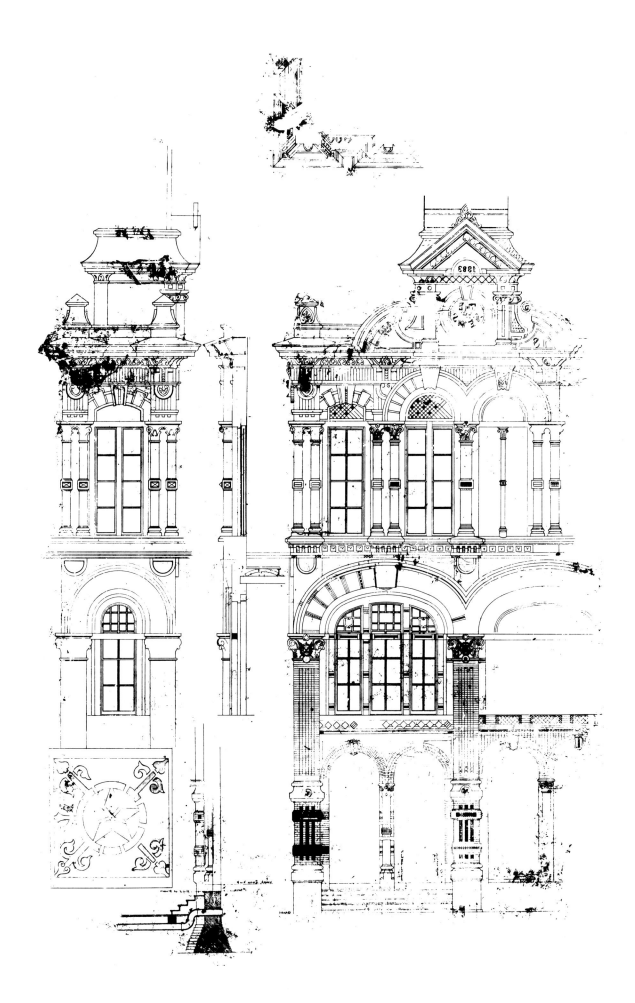

attracting a large portion of the city's population. The state Democratic convention was scheduled to be held there a few days after the fire, and the ruined building was to have housed many of the delegates and to have furnished space for some of the executive sessions. Visitors were crowded into downtown hotels, and clubs offered their quarters for meetings.

The Galveston News Building, 2108 Mechanic Street, 1883–84

Nicholas J. Clayton, Architect

The *Galveston* [*Daily*] *News*, until recently, was much more than a powerful local newspaper. It was the most influential paper in all of Texas, and its circulation on the mainland was larger than its city circulation.

The *News* was founded in 1842 by Michael Cronican and Wilbur Cherry, and Willard Richardson acquired control in 1843.[16] Under Richardson the newspaper prospered. Richardson visualized Galveston

as the apex of a vast transportation center through which the wealth of a "new empire" would flow to the world's markets; likewise, he saw the port as the ingress channel through which would pass the culture and products of the world to develop the vast interior. He saw Galveston as the "Queen City" and the *News* as the voice of the "Queen."[17]

In the fall of 1865, Colonel A. H. Belo, who had made a splendid record in the Confederate army and had come to Texas to better his fortunes, accepted the post of business manager. He proved an able coadjutor to Richardson and speedily "made his capacity felt."[k†] Later, John J. Hand, a "practical printer,"[l†] was added to management. Under these three, Richardson, Belo and Hand, the paper rapidly grew in circulation and patronage until it became the leading journal of the Southwest. As he grew older, Richardson entrusted the direction of the paper more and more to his younger partner, and at [Richardson's] death, Belo

THE GALVESTON NEWS BUILDING.
From original Clayton drawings.

bought his interest. Some time after, a Mr. Jenkins bought a share in the property; the firm became A. H. Belo & Company. Mr. Jenkins had been an editorial writer in New Orleans and had done part-time work for the *News*.

In 1881, a stock company was organized. On October 1, 1885, the *Dallas News* was established on a scale "benefiting the expansion" of that city by the principals in the Galveston company. The enterprise was remarkably successful. To quote one of its officers:

The Galveston *News* thoroughly supplied the section that could be reached easily from Galveston, and it was a question whether it should be satisfied with that sphere or should extend its news facilities to the most populous part of the state, by means of another newspaper. The result has been that, notwithstanding it was a time of depression, the Galveston *News* has, during the past year, received a full measure of the public support, and the Dallas *News* has just added so much more to the company's business. The relations of the two offices, by intermediate telegraphic service, etc., insures prompt publication of all that transpires, and the two newspapers are better enabled to employ a large editorial staff, so that matter can be written in Galveston or Dallas, according to the exigencies of publication.

The spirit of the times, as well as mere contemporary history, is ably reflected by this superior journal. It has the complete telegraphic service of two press associations, supplemented by its own specials from all the important news centers. Its presentation of events is full and impartial, and its mechanical equipment the latest and best in use.[18]

The handsome iron front at 2217 Avenue D had been built in 1858 by Willard Richardson as an interim plant for the *News*. Under the Belo administration of 1881, it was decided that a more impressive building was needed for the paper, and in 1883 Clayton was commissioned to build the structure at Twenty-first and Mechanic streets which was to serve the *News* for over eighty years.

Clayton's building is said to be the first ever designed especially for the publishing and printing of a newspaper. It is also asserted that when the *New York Times* built their structure on Forty-second Street and Seventh Avenue, the architects visited the Galveston News Building.

By 1883, Clayton was just beginning to feel confidence and freedom in the Romanesque. Almost gone are the remnants of Greek details. In their place is a plastic vigor and depth not seen in the earlier Clayton buildings. The windows are now deeply recessed from the face of the building, casting strong shadows on the southerly glass. The brickwork is as elaborate as in the Trueheart-Adriance Building but was done with a stronger, surer hand. The great arches within arches on the face of the building have the brutal detailing of the Norman twelfth century.

A line of columns runs down the length of the building to support the heavy weight of composing room and press. This is clearly expressed on the elevation. No architect has ever liked the idea of dividing his building in half vertically; architectural schools call it the first cardinal sin, but Clayton accomplishes it with great finesse.

The elaborate cornice, the last remnant of Clayton's Greek detailing, was destroyed in the storm of 1900, and the building today looks as if it had been part of a larger structure. The cornice had pulled the whole thing together, but the vigor and plastic quality of the building is enhanced without it.ᵐ† The News Building was completed in 1884; Thomas Lucas was the brickmason, and it is said to have cost $90,000.

The great Romanesque plastic elevation of the News Building was the forerunner and first draft of a much larger building to be built seven years later for the University of Texas Medical School. The same relationship exists between the Romanesque and modern architecture as links modern painting with primitive art. Picasso did not copy the patterns of African masks; he learned a new way of looking at his subjects from them. To a certain extent Clayton also found in the Romanesque not simply another transitory fashion but an affinity which aided him in moving toward the still hidden expressions of his own period.

When the News Building was built, the only waterworks system in the city was operated by a company that supplied salt water pumped from the bay. The pumping plant was located on the bay front at the foot of Twenty-sixth Street. Rainwater was collected for domestic use and to make steam. Thus, when the News Building was built, the entire basement was excavated and made into one huge brick cistern to contain the reservoirs of water required for the boilers and for other functions connected with the operation of the business.

The format of the newspaper, which prior to 1883 had been a folio with nine, ten or eleven long columns to the page, was changed to a quarto, originally with but six columns to the page and afterwards increased to seven columns; the number of pages grew to sixteen, twenty-four and as high as forty on Sundays. Ben Stuart, an old member of the staff, wrote in the April 11, 1917, *News*:

From 1884 to 1890–91 the paper was printed direct from type on a newly invented Hoe press, called in derision the "Dolly Varden," which for unreliability and a spoiler of paper was without a rival. After entailing the useless expenditure of a sum large enough to bankrupt the average newspaper it was eliminated and disposed of for a comparatively trifling sum in part payment for a new Seymour-Brewer press.

In this connection, it may be stated that the first seven-days-a-week morning newspaper in Texas was the original *Houston Post*, owned by J. W. Johnson and edited by Tobias Mitchell (from the *St. Louis Globe-Democrat*), which added a Monday morning edition in January 1883. The *Galveston News* immediately followed, and from that time to the present the paper has been printed every morning in the year with the exception of two periods of storm and stress when to do so was impossible.

Heidenheimer Castle, 1855.
Renovation in 1885
attributed to Nicholas J.
Clayton, architect.
Southwest corner and entry.
Ezra Stoller.

HEIDENHEIMER CASTLE.
SOUTHEAST CORNER AND ENTRY.
Ezra Stoller.

HEIDENHEIMER CASTLE.
DETAIL OF COLUMNS OF
DETACHED PORCH,
EAST ELEVATION.
Henri Cartier-Bresson, Magnum.

THE LANDES HOUSE, 1887.
DICKEY & HELMICH, ARCHITECTS.
EAST ELEVATION.
Ezra Stoller.

THE LANDES HOUSE.

DETAIL VIEW FROM PORCH.

Ezra Stoller.

THE LANDES HOUSE. DETAIL VIEW.
Henri Cartier-Bresson, Magnum.

Heidenheimer Castle, 1604 Avenue I, 1855

(Demolished 1974)[n][†]

Architect Unknown

Renovation in 1885—attributed to Nicholas J. Clayton

The castle is really two buildings. The original structure of 1855 included the square central portion, with four rooms on each floor, and was stylistically akin to the J. M. Brown House. In 1885 the tower was added.

The 1855 house was built by Colonel John S. Sydnor, an early mayor of Galveston,[o][†] the largest slave dealer in the state and a successful operator in all respects. The wall construction of the original house was of poured cement and oyster shell. The building is probably the second poured concrete structure in the U.S.

Colonel Sydnor, who came to Galveston from Virginia in 1838, was one of Galveston's most versatile, enterprising and public-spirited citizens. He had many "firsts" to his credit in addition to the concrete house. He was the first man to cultivate oysters in Galveston waters. While he was mayor, 1846–47, the city's police and fire departments were organized, and the first city market was built. His most progressive idea was a free public school system, which he was instrumental in establishing. After a few years of successful operation, it collapsed because the city aldermen failed to levy taxes for its support.

The house was purchased by B. T. Loring in 1869 and sold to Sampson Heidenheimer in 1884. In 1885 Mr. Heidenheimer completely renovated the building in the style of the eighties. It is probable that Nicholas J. Clayton was responsible for the renovation. There are no records to verify this, but the detailing of the bay windows has the same brutal vocabulary which Clayton was using and experimenting with at the time. Another clue can be found in the cast-stone columns of the attached porch on the east, similar to the cast-iron columns of the W. L. Moody Building of 1883, which Clayton designed.

Whether the attached porch was built as a "ruin" or not is difficult to assay. Ruins were the fashion of the day in the eastern United States and in Europe. It was particularly in the mode to have Greek or Gothic ruins in the garden carefully covered with moss. The Victorians adored buildings in a half-ruined state; they called it "pleasing decay."

The Heidenheimer family, including brothers Sampson, Abraham and Isaac, owned one of the largest grocery houses in Texas. Sampson, who was responsible for the renovation, owned the house from 1884 to 1890, Abraham from 1890 to 1894, [and] Louis Sonnentheil briefly from 1894 to 1895, when Abraham Heidenheimer again took possession. W. J. N. Hammons owned it in the year 1936, when he sold it to Raphael B. Munvine. In 1946 it was sold to James L. Korenek and in 1954 to Robert F. Wilburn. In 1962 Charlotte Ellen Warner bought it and is the present owner.

The building is now a rooming house in poor repair, particularly the interior. The central hall and stairway are famed for the very elaborate walnut detailing of the newel posts and balustrades. The dining room is covered with paneling which, if restored, might be presentable. Like almost all of Galveston's buildings, the main architectural effort was put into the exterior, and the interiors are as a rule disappointing, even when well maintained. A particularly interesting aspect of the building is that it was not raised during the grade raising of 1903–5.[p][†] The basement level assumes almost the proportion of a true basement, in that the fill has been laid close to the building, necessitating wells to clear the basement windows.

The Landes House, 1604 Avenue E, 1887

Dickey & Helmich, Architects[9†]

One of the strangest of the brick palaces is this house designed by the Houston and Galveston [architectural firm of Dickey & Helmich] and built in 1887. In style, it is under the strong influence of Richardson Romanesque—the brick and the general heaviness suggest the fortress that it is, unscathed by fire and flood to this day. Added was a mansard tower reminiscent of the high style of fifteen years earlier. An oriel perched on the south elevation apparently has been closed up from the beginning. Three tiny turrets originally crowned the southeast gable, and the chimneys appear to be ten feet too short for the fireplaces below to adequately draw. The cornices at the rooftop and the gable end are of architectural terra-cotta in the arabesque style of Louis Sullivan.

In addition, the lacy, double-columned two-story porch of cast iron faces the southeast corner wedged between the two extreme flanks of the building. The porch appears to be a compromise to Galveston's climate, but the rest of the building might well have been designed for the ferocity of a Boston winter.

The Landes House is not much appreciated architecturally today. The first reaction is disappointment. But if looked at more keenly, it is seen to be a handsome structure, dignified, and lyric.

The Romanesque Revival of which the Landes House is a late example, like all the other revivals in nineteenth-century American architecture, was based on earlier European revivals:

Like the other competitive styles, it spread rapidly and widely. It was used by builders and architects, famous and obscure, and ran its course for a quarter of a century. Its appeal was more direct than the Victorian Gothic. It seemed to be more earthy, pragmatic. It permitted variety and invention without becoming exotic or "fancy." It was picturesque, but rarely polychromatic.[19]

[The Dickey & Helmich firm] maintained offices in Galveston on the corner of Mechanic and Center streets. In 1887[r†] Andrew Morrison, in *The Industries of Galveston*, described how these gentlemen

. . . furnished the plans, and are now engaged in superintending the building of the new Union depot at Houston, which is to be of brick, and will cost from $75,000 to $100,000. Among other notable work which they are, or have recently been engaged on, may be mentioned the pressed brick residence of H. A. Landes, which will cost $30,000; the residence of H. O. Stein, $8,000; and that for George Schneider, Sr., which has cost $6,000. These are samples of the class of work they are entrusted with, and are illustrations of their skill and standing in their profession. Mr. Dickey has had many years experience as an architect, and Mr. Helmich, although still a young man, has displayed thorough knowledge of his vocation. They have been in partnership over a year.[20]

Landes was a wholesale grocer, liquor dealer, cotton factor and importer, whose office was on the Strand. From an account of the firm published in 1887 and "stripped of its verbiage":

Wallis, Landes & Company are one of the more prominent houses of Galveston. They do a cotton factorage and wholesale grocery business. They are a pioneer grocery house of the city. So far back as 1849 Messrs. J. C. and J. E. Wallis established a general mercantile business in Washington county, Texas, running in connection at the same time a large planting business which was continued up to the beginning of the war. Immediately after the close of the war, in 1865, the firm was organized under the style and firm name of Wallis, Landes & Co., the partners being J. C. Wallis, J. E. Wallis and H. A. Landes. In 1872 J. C. Wallis died, and his interest was withdrawn, J. E. Wallis and H. A. Landes becoming sole proprietors. The business, although one of the largest at the time of the succession of the present firm, has been materially enlarged by them during the twelve years they have controlled its operations, and to-day, taking into consideration the extent of its varied transactions, its spirited management and liberal

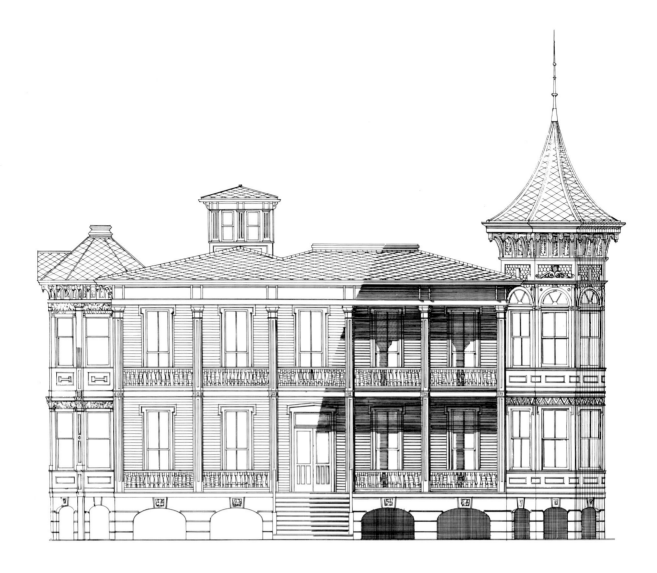

DARRAGH RESIDENCE, 1888–89.

ALFRED MULLER, ARCHITECT.

EAST ELEVATION.

Present-day ink drawing.

DARRAGH RESIDENCE.
EAST ELEVATION.
Ezra Stoller.

methods, must be rated with the most substantial houses not of Galveston alone, but of the South.

Transactions, including factorage and commission, and involving an annual aggregate of $2,000,000, with patrons in Texas, Louisiana, Arkansas, the Indian Territory and New Mexico, are recorded in the books of the house. The firm carries a full line of groceries, liquors and tobaccos, wooden and willow ware and other staples to the value of at least $150,000. To accommodate this stock a double-three-story brick building 43 x 120 feet is required. These premises are themselves an indication of the style in which they do business. They have been successful in their business and have acquired large resources whose character is illustrated by the following investments:

Mr. Wallis is a director of the Texas Banking and Insurance Company, vice-president and director of the National Bank of Texas, and a director in the Galveston Oil Company, and Gulf City Cotton Press; he is a large stockholder also in the Gulf, Colorado & Santa Fe Railroad. Mr. Landes is a director in the Texas Land and Loan Company, in the Galveston Real Estate and Loan Company, and other loan companies of the city. They are also engaged in real estate in the interior of the state, and are investors in the securities of nearly all the local corporations.

To this comprehensive sketch it seems unnecessary to add . . . [21]

The John L. Darragh Residence, 519 Fifteenth Street, 1888–89 [†]

Alfred Muller, Architect

John L. Darragh, president of the Galveston Wharf Company when he built his house in 1888–89, apparently joined together two existing smaller houses, as can be seen in the drawings, and added two towers and a cupola. It is difficult to date the two older structures which were completely rebuilt and absorbed by the larger struc-ture. A rather grand two-story Greek Revival portico of six columns was added to tie the two buildings together. The columns themselves, a modified Victorian version of the Greek, indicate the strength of the strange affair which Galveston carried on throughout the late nineteenth century with Greek form. There is an attempt in the addi-

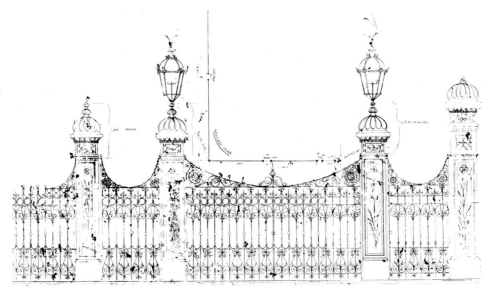

THE DARRAGH RESIDENCE.
From original working drawings of fence by Nicholas J. Clayton.

THE DARRAGH RESIDENCE.
BRICK WALL DETAIL.
Ezra Stoller.

tion of the two towers to straddle every taste and to be stylish at all costs. Both towers display the exuberance of wood Gothic by their handsome details, which include brackets, fish-scale shingles, and a wealth of architectural vocabulary. The curve of the octagonal roof of the north tower is particularly handsome.

Quite clearly the Darragh House called for the employment of an architect. However, the records are confusing as to who did the composite. Alfred Muller, who had probably come to Galveston in 1885, made some drawings for the house, but Nicholas Clayton wrote to the contractor in 1886 complaining about the quality of the wood used and the workmanship of the slate roof. From what little evidence there is, Alfred Muller should be credited with the Darragh House; Clayton was probably called in later to consult and supervise.[t†]

The cast-iron fence, which runs around two sides of the building and terminates in a brick and cast-stone fence to mark the property line, is a tour de force and still creates an impression. Muller's signed drawing for the fence is now deposited in the Rosenberg Library, as are the first- and second-floor plans of the house.[u†]

Darragh, as president of the Galveston Wharf Company, was an important factor in the policy-making tradition of the wharves. Andrew Morrison wrote:

Tradition substantiates the record in the statement that "so late as 1839 not a pier nor pile marked the harbor from Boliver Roads to Virginia Point," and that "vessels which occasionally cast anchor inside the bar had no accommodations whatever. The cargoes of vessels anchored in the stream were lightered ashore in small boats or rafts. This involved an expense and trouble that made it cheaper to transport goods by steamer to Houston, which, on that account, was the distributing point for the interior. It was evident that without landing facilities Galveston would never reach the dignity of a seaport. At this juncture the

Wharf Company was originated.

". . . The firm of Williams & McKinney constructed the first wharves on the bay front. Others were built soon after by Messrs. Menard, Sydnor, Jones, Captain A. P. Lufkin, Dr. Labadie and Mr. Bean; and these pioneer names are perpetuated in the titles of the wharves today. The Galveston Wharf Company originated in a consolidation of the interests of Messrs. Lufkin, Menard and Sydnor, which were merged into a single enterprise by a legislative charter obtained in 1854. The venture was hardly considered permanent, even so late as 1859, for but forty-four shares of stock had been issued to the ten subscribers who composed the company.

"In 1857 the city used the company to try the latter's title to its possessions on that portion of the bay front included within the streets, and in an elaborate opinion by Chief Justice Roberts, the Supreme Court of the state held that the titles of the original owners were vested in the assignees. A similar suit brought in 1868 resulted in a compromise between the litigants, whereby the city became a stockholder in the corporation and a participant in its profits." The schedule of rates formerly prevailing has been revised, and the charges upon commerce are now as reasonable as elsewhere.

[In 1886,] . . . the stock of the Wharf Company consisted of 26,266 shares, *and was* valued at $2,626,600. The company *paid* about $25,000 of city taxes yearly, beside those to the state and county. *Within ten years prior to 1886,* at least $250,000 *had* been expended by it in constructing new wharves, extending the old ones, dredging, filling flats, and improving the available wharf room, so that the company had accommodations to facilitate the discharge of more than a hundred sea-going vessels, conveniences ample for the trade of the port, and in continuous process of improvement as the city *grew*.[v† 22]

The house remained in the Darragh family until 1921, when it was sold to M. J. Tiernan. In 1926 it was sold to A. Trobis, and in 1928 Robert F. Stanton purchased the property. The building is now a rooming house with eight or ten marginal apartments in poor repair.

THE DARRAGH RESIDENCE.
NORTHEAST CORNER.
Ezra Stoller.

The Sonnentheil[w†] House, 1826 Avenue I, 1887

The Sonnentheil House stems directly from the Gothic Revival. The number of full-blown Gothic stone mansions was necessarily never very large; only wealthy men could afford such homes, which required the labors of highly skilled stone carvers. But the costly Gothic style could be translated into wood, and thousands of "carpenter Gothic" houses such as the Sonnentheil House still stand. This house was apparently constructed by a Galveston carpenter who spent years on its intricate lattice work. The carved heads, each representative of a different European nationality, below the Ionic capitals of the second-story porch were carved in Italy and shipped to Galveston especially for the builder. The name of the carpenter, an architectural genius, has long been lost.

Houses such as the Sonnentheil House were revolutionary. They marked the real beginning of modern architecture. The Greek Revival house was designed to fit behind a traditional façade, and it belonged in a formal garden. The Sonnentheil House breaks free from this academic scheme. It is planned from the inside out—the free layout of rooms determines the outward look; the picturesque exterior makes the most of sunlight, shade and foliage. It is a good house to walk around, to view at different times of the day and year. Inside, it has the happy quality of surprise.

Mr. and Mrs. J. Sonnentheil occupied the house from 1887 until 1911. In 1911, Mr. and Mrs. Charles Stubbs bought it and lived there until 1952, and it is still often referred to as the Stubbs House. In 1955 Jerry Barker, Galveston lawyer, bought it.[x†]

The Old City Hall, Twentieth Street and Mechanic, 1888

(Demolished 1966)[y†]

Alfred Muller, Architect

In 1846, with Galveston expanding, John Sydnor, the mayor, was looking to the future; the need for a city hall in which to transact the city's affairs was apparent, and the first city hall was constructed—a small wooden building on the north side of Market Street between Twentieth and Twenty-first streets. The city owned some property which was being used as a marketplace, where farmers from across the bay brought their produce to the city by boat. Sydnor conceived the idea of acquiring property upon which to build a large structure which could be used both as a city hall and a farmers' market. He proceeded to negotiate the sale of the market lots, and with the proceeds he purchased three lots on the west side of Twentieth Street extending from Market to Strand. Then he decided that the building, when erected, should be in the center of Twentieth

Street, with two narrow streets on each side.

Years passed, and the new city hall became a reality. The cornerstone was laid on the fifty-second anniversary of the Independence of Texas, March 2, 1888, by Lawrence Sullivan Ross, the nineteenth governor of Texas. A metal container was placed behind the cornerstone by Mayor Roger L. Fulton. Located under the east stairway at the northeast corner of the building, it bore the names of R. L. Fulton, Dan J. Buckley, city clerk, and the Committee of Public Property, James McDonald, chairman, Mose Ullman and W. S. Griffin.

Alfred Muller was the architect, and he declared the building his "masterpiece." Frank Jones was general contractor; he said it was one of the most elaborate and intricate he had ever constructed. But nothing of the great flamboyant spirit of this building remains. It was once a fine example of the French Renaissance, following by only eight years the Philadelphia City Hall.[z†] Like the Philadelphia City Hall, the ground-floor base is a highly rusticated firm foundation on which sits a myriad of columns, statues and architectural paraphernalia ranging from fourteenth-century English windows to sixteenth-century Italian balustrades and eighteenth-century American pilasters and garlands. Springing from the east and west corners of the south elevation were minaret-like round bays (oriels) rather precariously hung and crowned with mansard tile roofs and open flèches. The central tower had an open Palladian-motif pass-through below the clock. This gave the deep contrast of shadow which must have been spectacular under the glaring Texas sun.

The building was three stories high, with the farmers' market occupying the ground floor; the other two floors were city offices. The north portico, with its eight Ionic columns and decorated frieze, made an imposing sight. The grand stairways on the east and west sides made the building look even larger.

An important aspect was the belfry clock tower which rose 108 feet from the base of the building to the clock. Above the clock was a pinnacle thirty feet high. The huge windows above the second-floor arch were twenty-five feet high, and at the four corners of the tower stood four statues above the cornice, representing the spirits of Patriotism, Courage, Honor and Devotion. Below the clock was the decorated frieze. At the top of the building above the cornice, on both the east and west sides, there was also a varied array of statues, extending from the oriels at the corner of the building to the north end. This section of the building extended only 120 feet north from the tower.

The arches at the top of the stairway were sometimes used as a reviewing stand. The center arch on the north, with its heart-and-daggers design, still remains.

On September 2, 1901, the commission form of government was originated in the building. For the next sixteen years the building continued to be used as city hall until a new building was built in 1916. Since the removal of the city hall offices from the old site, the structure has been used for a police and central fire station, the farmers' market on the lower floor having long since been abandoned.

In the hurricane of 1900 the building, though severely damaged, was used as a refuge for the victims. Architecturally the building has been completely ruined since. The third story and tower have been removed and, where there had been statuary and other architectural motifs, signs designating the north section as the police department and the south section as the central fire station have been installed.

The Gresham House (The Bishop's Palace), 1402 Broadway, 1885–93[a‡]

Nicholas J. Clayton, Architect

Until very recently the most elaborate and imposing house ever built in Texas was the palace which Colonel Walter Gresham built for his wife, Josephine Mann Gresham. This was one of the most important commissions of the late eighties, and what little knowledge the world has of Clayton stems from this house, as it appeared in the centennial publication of the American Institute of Architects in 1957[b‡] as one of the one hundred important structures of the century 1857–1957.[c‡]

Colonel Gresham had intended to build the most elaborate house in Texas and he succeeded. The budget was astronomic for the era—no firm figure can be verified, but Clayton suggested that it had cost a quarter of a million dollars, and that figure has been contradicted as being $100,000 too low. Stylistically, it ranges through all the copy-

EXTREME LEFT, THE SONNENTHEIL
HOUSE, 1887.
Ezra Stoller.

books, from vague French Renaissance to Italian Romanesque, with a number of Galveston iron-work porches added on. Basically, the plan is a rectangle with the corners rising into four four-story towers topped with medieval and Renaissance tiled cones. The chimneys, real and false, are a major architectural element. They are so numerous that their silhouettes give the impression of a cluster of large houses—almost a town in themselves.

Perhaps nowhere, especially in cities of the East and in Europe, would such a large country house be built on such a small site. But it was characteristic of Texas, then and now, and visitors to Houston and Galveston are still amazed at the huge country-type houses built on town lots. Looking at the Gresham House, one can hardly get far enough away to get the full impact of the structure. Had there been a long drive up to the front of the house, the impression would have been magnified tenfold. The Fifth Avenue and Park Avenue houses of the same vintage were frankly town houses showing only the façade; this is a four-sided structure meant to be seen from all sides. Thus there was little limit to the details inside and out.

Materials on the exterior are native Texas granite, white limestone and red sandstone, all cut and shaped on the job. Leaded and stained-glass windows, elaborate carvings, at least two or three different kinds of roof tiles, free-standing cast sculptures and bronze dragons add to the splendor. Balconies appear from time to time, and the conservatory swells out from the east front facing Fourteenth Street. Over the entrance can still be seen the carved stone head of "Miss Beulah Gresham," the youngest daughter. Clayton had studied sculpture, and he drew the sketches for "Miss Beulah."

The Gresham House is one of the few Galveston houses in which considerable effort was put into the interior, but it still falls short of the refinements of the splendid Eastern or European town houses. The interior arrangements and finish were considered in Texas to be "the acme of taste and elegance."d‡ The main entrance on Broadway is approached by a flight of blue granite steps with random-work granite balustrades terminating in large newel posts of granite which formerly supported two large ornamental iron vases. Ascending the steps one observes two polished granite pillars supporting the archway. Massive oak doors are hung on rollers and slide back free from the entrance, revealing fully the wide hall which extends through the building and terminates in an octagon, from which the main stairway leads to the floors above.

Set in the walls of the octagon are three large stained-glass windows. A very elaborate mantel and gas-log fireplace, directly beneath the first landing, form a portion of the stairway. This mantel, like all the ornamental woodwork, was specially designed for the house. All the woodwork was hand carved. Three Venetian vases ornamented the mantel, while two large vases imported from Pisa stood on pedestals immediately in front and on either side of the fireplace. Around this octagonal portion of the hall were many panels of decorative tapestry painted by Mrs. Gresham.

The ceiling of the main hall, finished in oak, is supported by four polished Sienna-marble pillars on Numidian bases, two on either side, between which are French plate mirrors. Massive and elaborately carved double doors lead to the east into the library and dining room, to the west, into two large double parlors. The doors are finished on the hall side in oak and on the other sides to correspond with the finish of the rooms into which they lead. These doors could all be opened to make the entire main floor practically one vast room. Two sculptures of the period in Pyrian marble were placed in the main hall on the entrance side of the marble pillars.

The library, finished in carved curly walnut panels, contained well-filled cases of valuable books against every available foot of wall space. In this room was a large ornamental carved mantel and fireplace of Numidian marble. The corner fronting the two streets is circular, and contained potted ferns and rare plants. The dining room, probably the largest room in the house, was finished in antique oak. Elaborately hand-carved "jester" figures surmount each capital. Large sliding doors opened from the dining room into the octagon at the end of the main hall. At either side of the mantel are glass doors leading into the semicircular conservatory, which, like the library, was filled with rare ferns—a special section by Mrs. Gresham, who delighted in them and is said to have had one of the largest and most select collections in any private conservatory in the South.

The kitchen was Mrs. Gresham's special pride. It was a model of convenience equipped with all "modern" appliances, brass and copper trimmings, tile floor, etc. The kitchen was separated from the dining room by the butler's pantry and opened into the servant's hall, which connected with the rear yard and also opened into the dining room and main hall. From the servant's hall a winding stair and dumbwaiter (now an elevator) gave access to the two upper floors and to the basement. Immediately across the hall from the library to the left was the entrance of a drawing room finished in dark polished mahogany. The street end of this room is a bay window separated from the main room by an arch. On the west side is a magnificent mantel and fireplace of massive mahogany, heavily carved and polished. The walls were covered with gold satin damask, with gold beading.

The second parlor, larger than the first, was finished in white mahogany with satinwood trim. This room was decorated with silvery satin damask trimmed with silver beading. The decor included a prize mantel from a New Orleans exposition, made of Mexican onyx, silver and satinwood. On either side of the fireplace were double onyx columns with silver bases and capitals. Immediately above were solid silver fauns, about four feet tall, supporting additional onyx columns extending to the molding.

Colonel Gresham had come to Texas in 1866 from King's County, Virginia. He was a lawyer, educated at the University of Virginia, and had served in the Confederate army as one of "Lee's Rangers." He arrived in Galveston poor but with energy and perseverance soon built up a lucrative practice. He was one of the organizers of the Gulf, Colorado and Santa Fe Railroad and eventually became a U. S. Congressman.

The house remained in the Gresham family until 1923, when it was bought for $70,000 by the Roman Catholic diocese of Galveston, and for some years served as the palace of Bishop Christopher Byrne. During the latter years of his office, Bishop Byrne necessarily lived much of the time in Houston due to the growth of its part of the diocese; and Bishop Nolde, who succeeded Byrne, made little pretense of living in Galveston. The Gresham House, however, remained the official Bishop's residence until the early 1960s, when both residence and chancery were moved to Houston.[e‡]

The Lasker House, 1728 Broadway, 1889

(Demolished 1967)[f‡]

Nicholas J. Clayton, Architect

The Lasker House, one of Clayton's largest[g‡] private houses, is famous less because of its original owner, Morris Lasker, than because it was the childhood home of his son, Albert Lasker, one of the most extraordinary Americans of his time. The best account of his life is to be found in John Gunther's *Taken at the Flood: The Story of Albert D.*
Lasker. Sufficient for this description of his father's house is the fact that as president and owner of Lord & Thomas, an advertising agency which had begun in Chicago, Albert Lasker amassed a fortune, "by communicating abstractions,"[h‡] of $45 million, out of which he spent fabulous sums.

When the house was built in 1889, Morris

THE SONNENTHEIL HOUSE.
Henri Cartier-Bresson, Magnum.

Lasker, who had come to Galveston in 1869,[i‡] was the president of the M. Lasker Real Estate Company on Mechanic Street, between Twenty-first and Twenty-second streets. He had formerly been with the firms of Le Gierse & Company and Ullman, Lewis & Company, whose investments in lands, cattle and other ventures in Texas had made him one of the most notable men in Galveston. He was a director of the First National Bank, of the Island City Savings Bank and of several national banks in the interior, president of the Toyah Land and Cattle Company, and he was often chosen to represent the citizens at large in public matters of moment. The M. Lasker Company had been incorporated in 1886 for the purpose of dealing in improved city property in the booming towns of Texas, and had acquired some of the most valuable real estate in Dallas and other centers.[23]

The house was built of stuccoed brick with elaborate Romanesque details and a pastiche of details from all ages. The double-tiered porch to the southwest was a bow to local tradition added to the house. The stuccowork on the exterior has softened over the years and now has the doughlike quality which all Clayton's churches, chimneys and corners seem to have. The house, as one looks at the photograph, appears only vaguely the same as Clayton's drawings for the building. The tremendous detail shown in Clayton's drawings gives the appearance of late French Renaissance Revival palaces of New York and Paris. Today, the house, with its soft-gray stucco and its rounded edges, seems to have lost all of its detail. Some of the finials and lightning rods actually are gone, but there is a clear dichotomy between the building as designed and the building as it stands now. The Lasker House was built according to the drawings, but the three-dimensional result looks quite different.

The plan of the house suggests the good life of the late nineteenth century with its handsome, generous rooms and vertical circulation. Both back and front stairways are well to the rear of the house, allowing the ample reception hall on the ground floor to be unencumbered. The almost circular main stair leads to a particularly handsome upper hall, through which one reaches five bedrooms. Well-defined bathrooms and closets, sliding doors and an almost modern kitchen are all signs of the mature Clayton at his best.

The George Sealy House (The Open Gates), 2424 Broadway, 1886–91

McKim, Mead & White, Architects—Nicholas J. Clayton, Supervising Architect[i‡]

In the George Sealy House of 1886, the New York architectural firm of McKim, Mead & White turned from Neo-Colonialism entirely to the Italianate. In 1887, one year later,[k‡] they [were] commissioned to design the Boston Public Library, one of the great commissions in America, and there too they had turned entirely to the Italianate.

The Sealy House may very well be the last of the great romantic buildings stemming from the Richardson tradition. Could Stanford White, the designer, have felt that on the uncultured flats of Galveston there should be one last utterly romantic building? The narrow Roman bricks imported from Belgium, the garlands at the corners, the Italian Renaissance vases set about the building, the Palladian motif on the east elevation; all point to the Italian palazzo.

The result is a free adaptation of specific Italian precedents, not a slavish copy such as those shortly to emerge in the great Neo-Renaissance, Georgian and colonial revivals seen at the Chicago World's Fair of 1893. Though Italianate, though Renaissance, the Sealy House in its entirety and spirit is one of the last of the great romantic buildings of the nineteenth century.[l‡]

The J. C. Trube House, 1627 Avenue I, 1890

Alfred Muller, Architect

Two years after the Galveston City Hall was completed, Alfred Muller designed this strange small palace for J. C. Trube.

In an age when all houses faced the street, it took courage and inventiveness to design one whose entrance was at the corner of a block. The house plan breaks free from the academic schemes of the Greek Revival and the romantic revivals more than any other house in Galveston—certainly more than any of the great palaces. Essentially a raised brick cottage with a dormered and mansarded roof, this is the strangest house in a city of strange houses. The brick was stuccoed. The odd and exuberant abacuses which are seen above each column of the entry are probably structural corbels used to shorten the spans. The dormers are a collection which together give the appearance of an irregular pigeon roost. The tower on the north is a relatively traditional High Victorian Gothic expression. But the strangest element of all is the imitation chimney on the west front with a window through it announcing its lack of flue. Above the window are voluptuous volutes piled one on another—the entire complex of building dormers, stucco towers, corbels and carved lintels adds up to a neo-Garnier quality which perhaps can be found nowhere else in the world. Here is the ultimate expression of the wealth of exuberance and vigor of Galveston—of the willingness to venture forth borrowing bits and pieces from every style and coming up with a conglomerate which is essentially something new.

Although Muller never had the wide practice that was Clayton's, in the Trube house one can see that he was certainly a more daring and adventurous spirit—more willing to experiment.

The Trube house has been lived in continuously by the members of the Trube family, and Ozro W. Murphy, Jr., a great-grandson, occupies it now.[m‡] Mr. Murphy is the son of the late Etta May Nortdholtz Murphy, a granddaughter of Mr. and Mrs. Trube. The interior has been cut up into small apartments, and the original plan is all but unrecognizable. Like most of the Galveston houses, the interior falls far short of the exterior in design. It seemed that in Galveston's climate, where one could spend so much time outdoors, the big effort was put into the exterior. The factor of climate was probably combined with a basic urge for show at any price.

University of Texas Medical School, 916 Avenue B, 1890

Nicholas J. Clayton, Architect

One of Clayton's largest commissions, the Medical School probably looks better today than it did when its slenderized towerettes had a flèche to cap them and when there was a central octagonal turret on the top floor of the entry.[n‡] The most exciting aspect of the building is the extraordinary brickwork—above the arches and in the spandrels between the main and second levels, every other brick juts out to create a uniformly rough surface, perhaps never before so beautifully done. The red tile roof is a majestic affair rounding the two end bays perfectly, with the tiles adjusted for the much smaller circumference of the upper ridge of the roof. Romanesque is in full bloom in the Medical School.

Without question, Clayton was familiar with the great English architect R. Norman Shaw, whose work is still too little known to American architects. The large dividers which appear to be fire stops in the roof are unquestionably suggestive

OLD CITY HALL, 1888.
ALFRED MULLER, ARCHITECT.
SOUTH ELEVATION.
Photograph circa 1890.

LEFT: THE SONNENTHEIL HOUSE.
DETAIL, SOUTHWEST CORNER,
SECOND-STORY PORCH.
Henri Cartier-Bresson, Magnum.

OLD CITY HALL.
MORNING AFTER STORM OF
SEPTEMBER 1900.

[158]

OLD CITY HALL. SOUTH AND WEST
ELEVATIONS. THE THIRD FLOOR
TOTALLY REMOVED, THE ENTRY
PORCH GONE AND THE GREAT TOWER
REPLACED BY NEW, INSIGNIFICANT
CLOCK TOWER ADDED FOR FIREMEN'S
PRACTICE JUMPS.
Ezra Stoller.

THE GRESHAM HOUSE.
DETAIL, AT MAIN ENTRY.
Henri Cartier-Bresson, Magnum.

LEFT: THE GRESHAM HOUSE,
1885–93. NICHOLAS J. CLAYTON,
ARCHITECT. FRONT, SOUTH ELEVATION.
Ezra Stoller.

THE GRESHAM HOUSE.
DETAIL OF CONSERVATORY ROOF
AND EAST ELEVATION.
Henri Cartier-Bresson, Magnum.

THE GRESHAM HOUSE.
DETAIL, AT MAIN STAIRWELL.
Ezra Stoller.

THE GRESHAM HOUSE.
EAST, AND PARTIAL VIEW OF
NORTH ELEVATION.
Ezra Stoller.

THE LASKER HOUSE, 1889.
From original drawings of Nicholas J.
Clayton, architect.

THE LASKER HOUSE.
SOUTH AND EAST.
Ezra Stoller.

THE GEORGE SEALY HOUSE,
1886–91. McKim, Mead and
White, architects. East elevation with the Clayton carriage
house of 1891 in the far right
foreground.
Ezra Stoller.

THE GEORGE SEALY HOUSE.
SOUTH ELEVATION.
Ezra Stoller.

THE J. C. TRUBE HOUSE.
DETAIL OF WEST ELEVATION.
Henri Cartier-Bresson, Magnum.

THE J. C. TRUBE HOUSE, 1890.
ALFRED MULLER, ARCHITECT.
Henri Cartier-Bresson, Magnum.

UNIVERSITY OF TEXAS MEDICAL
SCHOOL, 1890.
Drawing circa 1895.

UNIVERSITY OF TEXAS MEDICAL
SCHOOL. DETAIL OF FRONT ENTRY.
Henri Cartier-Bresson, Magnum.

UNIVERSITY OF TEXAS
MEDICAL SCHOOL.
NICHOLAS J. CLAYTON,
ARCHITECT.
Ezra Stoller.

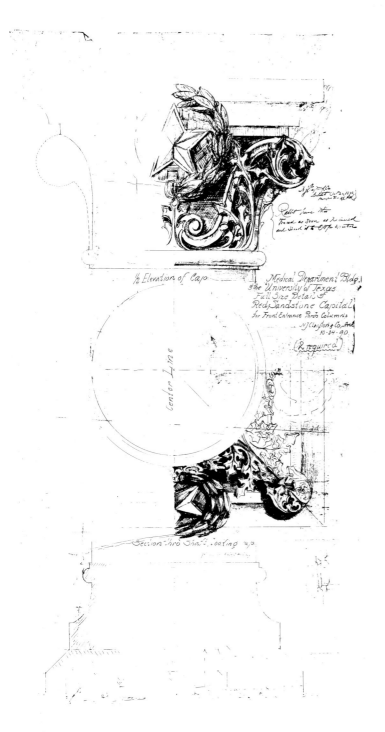

½ Elevation of Caps

Center Line

Medical Department Bldg.
The University of Texas
Full Size Details of
Red Sandstone Capital
for Front Entrance Porch Columns
N J Clayton & Co, Arch
10-24-90
(2 required)

Section thro' Shaft looking up

UNIVERSITY OF TEXAS MEDICAL
SCHOOL. DETAIL OF COLUMN
CAPITAL AT FRONT ENTRY.
From an original sketch by
Nicholas J. Clayton, architect.

UNIVERSITY OF TEXAS MEDICAL
SCHOOL. DETAIL OF FRONT ENTRY.
Henri Cartier-Bresson, Magnum.

[176]

University of Texas Medical
School. Detail.
Ezra Stoller.

URSULINE ACADEMY.
SOUTH ELEVATION.
Photograph circa 1896.

LEFT: URSULINE ACADEMY, 1891–94
(DEMOLISHED 1962). NICHOLAS J.
CLAYTON, ARCHITECT. DETAIL AT
FRONT ENTRY.
Photograph circa 1896.

of Shaw's Albert Hall mansions in London of 1879. This form, which seems to hark back to the Dutch Renaissance, appears again and again in Shaw's work. His New Scotland Yard, [built] just three years before the Medical School, has similar roof detailing, [which] appears also in the heroic-scaled Piccadilly Hotel in London of 1905.

The chief inspiration for the Medical School, however, is undoubtedly the work of H. H. Richardson, the great late nineteenth-century American architect. The detailing of the tower of Trinity Church (1873) in Boston is poorly repeated on the entry porch of the Medical School. The great two-story arches, which are the main motif of the building, probably stem from the Brown Thompson Department Store (also called the Cheney Block) built by Richardson in 1875. These forms, derivative as they are, are again and again

put together by the competent Clayton into new form. The buildings by Shaw and Richardson were decidedly asymmetric. Clayton, sensing the imminent Neo-Renaissance movement, here designed a symmetric structure.

The building is a refined and enlarged version of the Galveston News Building of seven years before. Two-story arches which looked incomplete on the News Building are a finished integral part of the Medical School. Final drawings of the school are almost the fulfillment of some early sketches for the News. The Medical School appears as something Clayton wanted to do on the News but could not, due to the confines of the site and the limited size of the earlier project. If there was the spark of genius in Clayton, it glows brightest in the Galveston News Building and its successor, the Medical School.

Ursuline Academy,°‡ 2600 Avenue N, 1891–94 (Demolished 1962)

Nicholas J. Clayton, Architect

The Ursuline Academy, without question Clayton's largest and most important commission, was demolished in 1962 after allegedly irreparable damage by the hurricane of September 1961. To architectural historians this was the greatest loss in a whole succession of losses. Whether the building really had to come down or not is now of little importance. Most architects feel it could well have been repaired and renovated to meet modern requirements, but we are still in the period of complete disregard for the great monuments built by our grandfathers. Philip Wylie, in an aggressive mood speaking of Victorian Washington, referred to the city as "dingy thoroughfares strewn with staggering edifices that present every sullen, rococo, snarling, sick, noxious and absurd form of *architectural design* in the long decades of Victorian false front."ᴾ‡ The Ursuline sisters may well have felt this same disregard, because of its historical overtones, for this magnificent monument to Victorian Gothic.

The Ursuline Academy was High Victorian

Gothic at its most elaborate, expensive, colorful and romantic. On the south was a two-story arcade connecting the convent with a lovely chapel. The succession of arched and foiled windows, deeply recessed to create sharp shadows in the subtropical sun, glittered, and the multicolored stones and brick were an endless mosaic—a magnificence never before or since attempted in Texas. The brick and stonework of the piers, the colonnettes and the vaults were richly treated in a fashion as much polytonal as polychromatic. The banding was in bricks and stones of different sizes and textures as well as different colors. Here was the supreme monument, in a style with which Clayton was most familiar. He worked here with a deftness of hand not seen in any of his other buildings, and his flair for Gothic—particularly Venetian Gothic—detailing and proportion is masterful. Above all, being the Gothic Revivalist he was, Clayton saw to it that the craftsmanship was excellent throughout. Here was a very large building, isolated where it could be seen from a distance, and the carefully studied silhouettes were varied by towers and other skyline features to enhance its scale.

The convent was established in 1847 by Bishop J. M. Odin, aided by six nuns from New Orleans. Within a decade it housed a flourishing day and boarding school, and it later served as a hospital through yellow fever epidemics. During the Battle of Galveston the Ursuline nuns refused General Magruder's offer of transportation to a safety zone and maintained in the convent a hospital for the wounded of both armies. Young Lieutenant Sidney A. Sherman, son of General Sidney Sherman, died here.

Federal forces, mistaking the convent for a Confederate stronghold during the battle, concentrated their fire on it. General Magruder sent word to the sisters to hoist a yellow flag, the signal for quarantine. Shells fell closer as the gunners on the ships improved their range, while the sisters hunted frantically for yellow cloth. Local tradition says that one of them found a wide yellow skirt in a student's trunk, that a soldier climbed to the belfry and waved it aloft and that the bombardment stopped immediately. For years afterward the sisters picked up spent shells on the grounds and used them for flatiron stands, until one exploded and shattered a wall of the laundry.[24]

The Willis-Moody House, 2618 Broadway, 1894

W. H. Tyndall, Architect

Mrs. Richard S. Willis hired W. H. Tyndall, a Galveston architect, to design her palace at 2618 Broadway in 1894. Her husband and his brother, P. J. Willis, had been successful cotton factors and importers of groceries and dry goods since 1837, the year before Galveston was founded. They had come to Galveston from Maryland at the same time as [Michael B.] Menard. At first, they ran a modest merchandise business, but it expanded with the growth of the city. By the 1870s, the firm was among the largest of the local merchants and, in fact, was one of the larger wholesale firms in America. The business was on the Strand, occupying almost an entire block. Andrew Morrison, writing in 1887, speaks of two connecting brick structures—one 120 feet by 128 feet, four stories high; the other 86 feet by 120 feet, three stories high—with a total floor space of over 100,000 square feet.[25] These buildings had steam elevators, and there was a private railroad siding at the rear of the mammoth establishment where railroad cars could be loaded with merchandise for shipment to customers throughout Texas, Louisiana and Mexico. Of all the merchandising firms operating in Galveston, this was perhaps the oldest.

It was small wonder that Tyndall, the architect, planned an imposing palace. The contractor was Harry Devlin, who built many of the large projects of the time.

The circumstances under which W. L. Moody, Jr., purchased the house on September 15, 1900, six days following the disastrous hurricane, are legendary. It is said that it was bought for $20,000 or "ten cents on the dollar," which, in this case, may be a figure of speech but also may be an accurate description of a transfer of property.[‡] Whether the Willis family completely lost confidence in the future of Galveston and were willing to sell out at an absurd price, or whether the affairs of P. J. Willis & Company were on the decline, or whether there were personal reasons not now known to explain the transaction is speculation. Certainly Colonel Moody and W. L. Moody, Jr., strongly opposed abandoning the city, an idea proposed by some discouraged citizens following the storm. W. L. Moody, Jr., recalled that his father had said to him following the storm, "We both like to fish and hunt; if they do abandon the city, remember, the fewer the people, the better the fishing."[26] This statement has been interpreted in a number of ways. Some consider it to be the key to the decline of Galveston.

Tyndall produced none of the elaborate detailing which Clayton had used in his palace for the Greshams six years before. The Willis-Moody House is solemn and grave. The turrets and dormers and arches do nothing to relieve what is, in fact, a grim, pedestrian, expensive pile. The fantasy and exuberance of Clayton is nowhere to be found.

Tyndall certainly took a long look at Stanford White's Sealy House, however, and the arches on the main level, the protruding southwest tower—even the detailing of the chimneys and the weather vanes—are similar. He produced a lavish and expensive house of red brick and Texas limestone and a red tile roof with some structural advances. There is an indication that structural steel was used to help support the floors—a first for houses in Texas. The kitchen, cold-storage rooms, laundries, wine cellars, furnace rooms, etc., on the ground floor indicate a serious approach to utilitarian problems, a factor not common to the era.

Pottier Stymus & Company of New York were the decorators of the more than thirty rooms. Tiled floors contrasted with solid mahogany ceilings.

Like so many of the houses of the era, rare woods were used for hand-carved paneling, mantelpieces, friezes and sideboards. Grained satinwood was used for the arch mantel and beamed ceilings of the living room. The entry hall, including its beams and ceilings, is paneled in oak. The library is mahogany. On the landing of the stairway was set a huge semireligious stained-glass window of pseudo-Renaissance pretensions but of unfortunate perspective and draftsmanship. This is believed to have been imported from Vienna.

East of the entry hall is the typical ballroom and reception room, with ornate and elaborate gold-leaf mirror stands and carefully painted-out plaster cornice detailing. None of the rooms is very impressive except the dining room, which is magnificent in scale, with a coffered gold-leaf metal ceiling and an elaborate two-foot frieze running round the walls.

With all its pretension, the Willis-Moody House ends up as the least inventive and the least beguiling of the great Galveston houses.

Since the death of W. L. Moody, Jr., the house has been occupied by Mr. Moody's daughter, Mrs. Mary Moody Northen.[r‡]

Sacred Heart Church, Fourteenth Street and Broadway, 1903–4

Brother Jimenez, S. J., Architect

Clayton's Sacred Heart Church, so damaged in the hurricane of 1900, was redesigned and rebuilt in 1903–4 by a Jesuit brother named Jimenez. Why Clayton did not receive the commission to rebuild Sacred Heart is a story which may never be known. It is said that in order to save money, a member of the clergy was employed to avoid an architectural commission.[27] This may very well have been the case; however, the fact that Clayton, a well-esteemed Catholic and an architect who had built the great monuments of the city, was not commissioned would indicate that his career was waning. Yet Clayton, in 1903, was only sixty-two years old.[s‡]

Almost nothing is known of Brother Jimenez's career as an architect. He is said to have built a similar church in New Orleans close to the present Roosevelt Hotel. The style of the new Sacred Heart Church is anachronistic and out of place in architectural history.[t‡] The Byzantine and Hindu themes had fallen out of high fashion thirty years before, and the very window detailing and foiling is reminiscent of the Congregation B'nai Israel Synagogue of almost thirty-five years earlier. In the early 1900s, when the quiet and elegant return to academic early Gothic was the vogue for tasteful churches, Jimenez designed a flamboyant and bizarre building which today, completely whitewashed, looks almost like an operatic stage set. The distinct impression is the papier-mâché decor of the pastrycook's art.

In 1915 Nicholas J. Clayton added a more impressive dome to the church, which survived unscathed another devastating hurricane in August of that year.[u‡] He raised and enlarged the dome, adding the almost onion-shaped protuberance which now graces the building. Its flying buttresses, to meet the thrust of the dome, are far too low to be effective, but one can well understand why Clayton's heart was not in the work. Clayton was seventy-four.[v‡] He must have suffered deeply from the decline in his career.

The Sweeney-Royston House, 2402 Avenue L, 1885

This house was built for the son-in-law and daughter, Matilda E. Sweeney, of J. M. Brown. Mrs. Sweeney occupied the house from 1885 to 1905, and it was owned from then until 1911 by J. H. W. Steele. Judge Mart H. Royston lived in the house from 1911 until 1954, hence its name. From 1954 to 1955 it was owned by the Trinity Episcopal Church. Lloyd F. Sanborn owned it from 1955 to 1960, and Dr. Herndon H. Clarke has owned it since.[w‡]

The Sweeney-Royston house is attributed to Nicholas J. Clayton by his daughter, Miss Mary Clayton, although no corroboration has been found. Note the mariner's-wheel detail of the porch balustrade, a slightly different version of which also appears on the McDonald House (1890), 926 Avenue G.

The Reymershoffer House, 1302 Avenue E, 1886–87[x‡]

The house of Gus Reymershoffer is attributed to Nicholas J. Clayton by his daughter, Mary Clayton. No corroboration has been found. The house is not particularly distinguished except for the porch columns, the thinness of which seems to be an attempt to imitate in wood the slender quality of the cast-iron columns so common in Galveston. Here is the virtuosity of the carpenter: the heavy third-story gable end appears as a great weight sitting on the delicate wood columns.

The Reymershoffers in 1887 were extremely successful grain merchants with an elevator storage capacity of 300,000 bushels. Gus Reymershoffer with his brother, J. Reymershoffer, in their Texas Star Flower [*sic*] Mills had a daily production capacity of over 800 barrels in rye and wheat flour.

The McDonald House, 926 Avenue G, 1890

Originally built by Liberty S. McKinney, the house was sold in 1905 to J. L. Boddeker, who sold it in 1907 to D. D. McDonald. The McDonald family has occupied it since.[y‡]

In addition to the striking porch, with its pearl-drop pendants and mariner's-wheel details within the elaborate undulating arches, there was on the original building a multicolored and impressive tile roof. If there was an architect, he is unknown. The design of the building is probably the work of carpenters, influenced by their copybooks as well as [by] the local porch traditions of the Galveston style. The influence of the Trube House, built by Alfred Muller in the same year, is also evident.

THE WILLIS-MOODY HOUSE.
DETAIL OF LION'S HEAD AT FRONT
ENTRY.
Henri Cartier-Bresson, Magnum.

THE WILLIS-MOODY HOUSE, 1894.
W. H. TYNDALL, ARCHITECT.
Ezra Stoller.

[187]

THE WILLIS-MOODY HOUSE.

Ezra Stoller.

SACRED HEART CHURCH (II), 1903–4.
BROTHER JIMENEZ, S.J., ARCHITECT.
Ezra Stoller.

SACRED HEART CHURCH.
*Present-day sketch showing original dome
of 1903-4.*

SACRED HEART CHURCH (II).
Henri Cartier-Bresson, Magnum.

THE SWEENEY-ROYSTON HOUSE,
1885.
Ezra Stoller.

THE SWEENEY-ROYSTON HOUSE.
DORMER DETAIL, EAST
ELEVATION.
Henri Cartier-Bresson, Magnum.

The Lucas Apartments, 1407–9 Broadway, 1901–8[z][‡]

These apartments were built by the successful brick contractor Thomas Lucas after his earlier apartment project, at a location slightly closer to the beach, had been destroyed in the 1900 storm. The original building was said to have been the first in Galveston specifically built as apartments. The strange coral-and-shell, window-boxed balconies are a provincial and spontaneous example of the great Art Nouveau movement of the era.

Post Office Street, West of Twenty-fifth Street

Among the glories of Galveston until the late 1950s were the famed bordellos along several blocks of Post Office Street west of Twenty-fifth Street. They are not particularly distinguished for their architecture except for the latticework porches by which the initiated could identify them.[a][•]

Notes

1. Biographical sketch of Nicholas J. Clayton (1840–1916), records of the American Institute of Architects, Washington, D. C.

2. George E. Pettengill, librarian of the American Institute of Architects, to author, 1 August 1963.

3. Morrison, *The Industries of Galveston*, 121.

4. Kempner, 1.

5. *Galveston [Daily] News*, 6 February 1928.

6. Morrison, *The Industries of Galveston*, 80.

7. Ibid., 74, 77.

8. Ibid., 82.

9. Ibid., 80.

10. Ibid., 79.

11. *House of Moody Magazine* (September 1933): 17.

12. Green Peyton Wertenbaker, *The Face of Texas, A Survey in Words and Pictures* (New York: Bonanza Books, 1961), 242.

13. *Galveston Tribune*, 1 July 1933.

14. Kempner, 24–25.

15. Ibid.

16. Fornell, *The Galveston Era*, 142.

17. Ibid., 145.

18. Morrison, *The Industries of Galveston*, 72–73.

19. Carroll L. V. Meeks, "Romanesque Before Richardson in the United States," *Art Bulletin*, 35, no. 1 (March 1953): 32.

20. Morrison, *The Industries of Galveston*, 115.

21. Ibid., 82–83.

22. Ibid., 53–54.

23. Ibid., 115.

24. *Galveston [Daily] News*, 19 January 1937.

25. Morrison, *The Industries of Galveston*, 88.

26. W. L. Moody and Company, *Three Quarters of a Century of Progress* (pamphlet).

27. From notes given the author by Miss Mary Clayton, daughter of Nicholas J. Clayton, in Galveston, Texas, 1963.

a. Whorton-Fox erratum.

b. Whorton-Fox erratum.

c. Whorton-Fox erratum.

d. Whorton-Fox erratum.

e. Whorton-Fox erratum.

f. See chapter 1, note b.

g. A. W. N. Pugin, *The True Principles of Pointed or Christian Architecture: Set Forth in Two Lectures Delivered at St. Marie's Oscott* (London: John Weale, 1841), 23.

h.	The building has been renovated and now houses shops. It has been sold by Flood and Calvert.

i.	Whorton-Fox update. Because the building was demolished, some of the following descriptive text is obsolete.

j.	Whorton-Fox update. Because the building was demolished, some of the following descriptive text is obsolete. The date of demolition was not given in the errata list, but it obviously occurred between 1966, the book's publication date, and 1977, when the errata list was compiled.

k.	Because the building was demolished, some of the following descriptive text is obsolete.

l.	A. J. Downing, *The Architecture of Country Houses*, sec. 1 (New York: D. Appleton and Company, 1850), 37–38. Quoted in John Gloag, *Victorian Taste*, vol. 1 (Newton Abbott: David and Charles, 1979), 62.

m.	Whorton-Fox erratum.

n.	Whorton-Fox erratum.

o.	Whorton-Fox erratum.

p.	Whorton-Fox erratum.

q.	Morrison, *The Industries of Galveston*, 74.

r.	The building has undergone major renovation.

s.	Whorton-Fox erratum.

t.	Whorton-Fox erratum.

u.	Beasley notes: "The Junior League bought the building and did a major renovation; their offices are here. This was the *first* building to have been renovated on the Strand, and the League has never been given the credit it deserves."

v.	In their errata list, Whorton and Fox reject the attribution to Nicholas Clayton included in the first edition, which, according to the author, was based on a personal interview with Miss Mary Clayton, Clayton's daughter. The following text has been edited slightly to reflect this change.

w.	See chapter 1, note b.

x.	Kempner, 2.

y.	It is not certain that W. L. Moody, Jr., wrote this passage. The article "First Moody Building Observes Its Golden Anniversary" was published anonymously, and in it, Moody is quoted at length. See note z, which follows, for full bibliographic information.

z.	"First Moody Building Observes Its Golden Anniversary," *House of Moody Magazine* (September 1933): 17.

a†.	The building now houses Colonel Bubbie's Army Outlet. There has been some exterior renovation.

b†.	Should be July 1, 1883.

c†.	*Galveston Daily News*, 1 July 1883. Quoted in Lillian Rice, "Beach Hotel, Pride of Treasure Island, Opened Fifty Years Ago; Galveston's First Big Development Along Tourist Resort," *Galveston Tribune*, 1 July 1933.

d†.	Ibid.

e†.	*Galveston Daily News*, 1 July 1883.

f†.	Rice.

g†.	Ibid.

h†.	Ibid. Italics added. Author interpolation. Rice writes, ". . . secured in Beaumont, Tex. and from the lobby to the kitchen no detail was omitted that might add attractiveness or comfort. The kitchen was a two-story building detached from the hotel. This plan was followed in order to lessen the possibility of fires." The Rice quotation ends here. The next two sentences constitute an interpolation by the author.

i†.	Source of quotation unknown.

j†.	Source of quotation unknown.

k†.	Source of quotation unknown.

l†.	Hayes, *Galveston: History of the Island and the City*, 695.

m†.	Beasley notes: "The façade has been covered over, and the building has been defaced but is standing. It is undergoing a slow death as opposed to demolition."

n†.	Whorton-Fox update. Because the building has been demolished, some of the following descriptive text is obsolete.

o†.	Whorton-Fox erratum.

p†.	See chapter 1, note b.

q†.	Whorton-Fox update. In the first edition, the building was attributed to architect George E. Dickey, rather than to his firm. The following descriptive text has been edited slightly to reflect the change. The house was purchased in 1993 by Chris McCasland and is undergoing restoration.

r†.	Whorton-Fox erratum.

s†.	Whorton-Fox erratum. The following descriptive text has been altered slightly to reflect this correction. The building burned around 1991.

t†.	Whorton and Fox write, "Subsequent research has clarified this obscurity. Darragh in 1886 had Clayton design a house for him at 1827 Avenue F. In 1888, Darragh's third wife, Laura Leonard Darragh, had Alfred Muller design the house on Fifteenth Street, completed in 1889. While the house was under construction, Judge Darragh was declared insane and committed to the care of his wife."

u†. Whorton-Fox update.

v†. Italics added. Author interpolation. Morrison writes, ". . . is nominally valued at $2,626,600. The company pays about $25,000 of city taxes yearly, beside those to the state and county. During recent years at least $250,000 have been expended by it in constructing new wharves extending the old ones, dredging, filling flats, and improving the available wharf room so that the company had accommodations to facilitate the discharge of more than a hundred sea-going vessels, convenience ample for the trade of the port, and in continuous process of improvement as the city grows." 53–54.

w†. Whorton-Fox erratum. "Sonnentheil" was spelled "Sonnenthiel" in the first edition.

x†. The building now has a different owner.

y†. Whorton-Fox update. Because the building has been demolished, some of the descriptive text is obsolete.

z†. The Philadelphia City Hall was constructed between 1871 and 1881. Architects were John McArthur, Jr., and Thomas U. Walter.

a‡. Whorton-Fox erratum.

b‡. Whorton-Fox erratum.

c‡. Whorton-Fox erratum.

d‡. Source of quotation unknown.

e‡. It is still owned by the Church and is open as a house museum.

f‡. Whorton-Fox update. Because the house has been demolished, some of the following descriptive text is obsolete.

g‡. Whorton-Fox erratum.

h‡. Source of quotation unknown.

i‡. Whorton-Fox erratum.

j‡. Whorton-Fox erratum. The following descriptive text has been edited slightly to reflect the corrected construction date and spelling of McKim, Mead & White.

k‡. Whorton-Fox erratum.

l‡. The building was bequeathed to the University of Texas Medical Branch by George Sealy, son of the builder. It has undergone major renovation.

m‡. The house has changed ownership since publication of the first edition. It has undergone major renovation.

n‡. The building is called "Old Red." It has undergone major renovation by the University of Texas.

o‡. Whorton-Fox erratum. The following descriptive text has been edited slightly to reflect the corrected building name.

p‡. Italics added. Author interpolation. Wylie writes, ". . . every sullen, rococo, snarling, sick, noxious and absurd form of vainglorious house and apartment architecture designed in the long decades of Victorian false front." Philip Wylie, *Generation of Vipers* (New York: Rinehart and Company, 1955), 267.

q‡. Whorton and Fox write, "It now appears that local legend was exaggerated, for when Mrs. Willis died in September 1899, her house was valued at $40,000, although it was reported as costing twice as much to build five years earlier. Mrs. Willis' estate was involved in litigation, and most of her heirs no longer lived in Galveston, contributing to the supposition that the Willis family was eager to sell the huge house."

r‡. The building has been restored and opened as a house museum.

s‡. Whorton-Fox erratum.

t‡. Whorton and Fox write, "The newly installed Rector of the church directed that it be patterned after the Immaculate Conception Church in New Orleans (of mid-nineteenth-century 'Moorish' design), the mother church of the Jesuit province in the South. Contemporary reports in the Galveston newspapers also cite a Puerta Santa Maria in Spain as the ultimate model."

u‡. Whorton-Fox erratum.

v‡. Whorton-Fox erratum.

w‡. Since publication, the house has changed ownership and undergone major renovation.

x‡. At the suggestion of Whorton and Fox, the attribution of Nicholas J. Clayton as architect has been dropped from the text.

y‡. The building underwent major renovation but was damaged by fire in 1992 or early 1993. The building has recently been sold and will be restored again.

z‡. Whorton-Fox erratum.

a•. Some have been demolished since publication of the first edition.

THE REYMERSHOFFER HOUSE,
1886–87.
Ezra Stoller.

THE REYMERSHOFFER HOUSE.
Henri Cartier-Bresson, Magnum.

THE MCDONALD HOUSE, 1890.
Henri Cartier-Bresson, Magnum.

THE MCDONALD HOUSE.
PORCH DETAIL.
Henri Cartier-Bresson, Magnum.

THE LUCAS APARTMENTS, 1901–8.
Ezra Stoller.

THE LUCAS APARTMENTS.
Henri Cartier-Bresson, Magnum.

BORDELLO ON POST OFFICE STREET,
WEST OF TWENTY-FIFTH STREET.
Henri Cartier-Bresson, Magnum.

Epilogue

Galveston is the most important seaport in Texas, and nothing can retard its commercial prosperity. Its rapid improvements, says one of the chronicles of the day, have been unequalled in the annals of town-making. Blessed with a harbor equal, if not superior to any on the Gulf, with a climate mild and generally healthy, it cannot fail to attract the attention of capitalists. It must be the great mart whence all our foreign shipments are to be made; and the prosperity of other cities on the coast, not so blessed with good harbors, so far from injuring Galveston, will add to its importance. When Texas shall become densely settled, and the resources of the country brought out, Galveston will enjoy a richer commerce, and ship a larger amount of cotton than any other city in America. This may appear an extravagant declaration to those unacquainted with the country, but when we reflect that the whole region from the Sabine and Trinity to the Rio Grande, a distance of more than seven hundred miles, comprises the richest cotton, sugar, and tobacco country, the richest farming and grazing district in the world, the assertion will not appear gratuitous.

Galveston, like Tyre, is built upon an island in the midst of the sea, and if her people, like the Tyrians of old, continue to be economical, industrious, and enterprising; sincere, faithful, and hospitable to strangers; if they maintain a good police, free trade, and are faithful to their engagements; if they punish fraud and reward virtue; if they are not inflated by avarice and pride on the one hand, nor enervated by luxury and idleness on the other; she will become the centre of commerce, the resort of all nations, and attain the wealth and power, and it may be, as we have elsewhere predicted, the greatness and glory of the ancient city.

—A. Suthron, *Prairiedom: Rambles and Scrambles in Texas or New Estrémadura* (1846)

christ but they're few

all (beyond win
or lose) good true
beautiful things

god how he sings

the robin (who
'll be silent in
a moon or two)

—e. e. cummings
73 Poems

Afterword

The Galveston That Was: Requiem or Inspiration?

In August 1987, Howard Barnstone, respected architect and author of *The Galveston That Was*, died unexpectedly in Houston. After the immediate shock and sorrow, I found my thoughts turning again and again to this beautiful and haunting book. This single volume, published in 1966, succeeded in galvanizing strong public interest in the disappearing architecture of Galveston and continues to inspire preservation programs today.[1]

In the 1950s and early 1960s there remained in Galveston one of the finest collections of nineteenth-century architecture in the United States. Some three hundred blocks of the island city were packed cheek-by-jowl with hundreds upon hundreds of Victorian structures.

In the residential areas, high above their compact yards, sat raised cottages, intricate frame houses and imposing mansions. They presented a dazzling array of porches, double galleries, crazy-quilt rooflines cut by multiple dormers, grand entryways with massive ten-foot-high doors, beveled and stained glass and rusticated stucco on piers and chimneys. Those built of wood were accented—even frosted—with elaborate patterns of millwork, giving rise to the popular term "Carpenter Gothic" to describe this vernacular exuberance.

In the adjacent commercial area, three- to seven-story buildings rose in ornate walls along sidewalks already raised well above the level of the streets. Cast-iron columns, running arches, rhythmic rows of tall cypress doors and polychrome brick set in planes of detailing enlivened the façades. High above, massively ornate cornices added as much as another story to the building height.

These structures represented the dreams of European immigrants, who saw in the promised land of Galveston and Texas the opportunity to build for themselves the castles, chateaux and ornate stone masterpieces so familiar, yet so unobtainable, in their homelands. Never mind the lack of stone and stonemasons in this new city on its island of sand; with characteristic tenacity they built in brick, then covered the brick with stucco and finally rusticated it all to look like stone—or, more frequently, they simply recreated the glories of carved stone out of wood, paint and carpentry genius.

These structures came into being in Galveston in the mid and later 1800s during the time that Galveston was the commercial center of Texas— the largest, wealthiest and most cosmopolitan city in the state. Indeed, some sources attribute to Galveston the second highest per capita wealth of any city in the United States in the 1890s. Galvestonians amassed wealth and, with their newly created affluence, designed and constructed houses and buildings to match their dreams—or, almost as good, to impress their neighbors.

Many of these structures were destroyed in the great hurricane of September 8, 1900. Maps show nearly fifty percent of the city's blocks— mostly those on the Gulf side of the island—virtually wiped clean. And yet so many structures had filled the city that an amazing quantity survived the 1900 storm.

In the years immediately following the storm, the massive seawall was constructed, and in an equally miraculous engineering feat, the grade level of most of the city was actually raised, as much as eight or nine feet in some areas. With these new safeguards, the thousands of remaining structures were able to survive subsequent storms.

The other event essential to these structures' continuing survival was, ironically enough, Houston's opening of its ship channel in 1914 and the shift of commercial momentum from Galveston to Houston and other Texas ports. Having lost its deep-water monopoly, Galveston fell back on the bootlegging, gambling and prostitution already rife in the city as an economic mainstay. Despite the allure of these attractions, Galveston experienced virtually no economic or population growth through mid century. With this lack of growth came the survival of the older structures, many of which, in a more dynamic economy, would have been cleared for new construction.

Then in 1956–57, the Texas attorney general and Texas Rangers, smashing an estimated twenty-five hundred slot machines, finally succeeded in closing down the gambling industry in Galveston and with it many of the prostitution and illegal liquor-by-the-drink establishments. With gambling shut down, Galveston temporarily hit rock bottom while it struggled to find its economic future in other directions.[2]

In the midst of these turbulent changes, intensified by heated disputes as the city moved from racial segregation to integration, almost no one perceived the importance of Galveston's treasury of historical structures.

Almost no one. Amidst a community largely oblivious to these architectural treasures, two gallant exceptions existed. First, in 1954, a small cadre of strong-willed citizens led by Mrs. Paul Brindley saved the Williams-Tucker House from destruction. At the same time, they incorporated the 1871 Galveston Historical Society as the Galveston Historical Foundation and expanded its statement of purpose from saving documents important to Texas and Galveston history to saving historic landmarks.[3]

Second, in 1962, a group including State Representative Maco Stewart succeeded in having the Old Galveston Quarter Act passed by the Texas legislature and signed by the governor. The act empowered a five-member commission to protect structures within a forty-block section of Galveston's East End.[4] This, however, required the support of a majority of property owners within the area, and, unfortunately, in a special election in 1963, the proposal was defeated by nearly a two-to-one margin.[5]

Aside from these two heroic efforts, one saw widespread neglect and deterioration slowly destroying Galveston's historical structures in the 1950s and 1960s.

Howard Barnstone and the Book's Origins

In 1948 Howard Barnstone moved to Houston to become a lecturer in architecture at the University of Houston. Barnstone had grown up in Maine, graduated from Yale College and then obtained a master's degree in architecture from Yale University. In 1953 he married a talented Houston artist, Gertrude Levy, who recalls how her husband "was simply bursting to explore and absorb all of Texas that he could." Barnstone loved the warm Texas sun after the cold winters of Maine, and he and his wife soon discovered Galveston. They would drive up and down street after street, exploring the old structures and delighting in the unending vernacular interpretations of Victorian styles.

Barnstone loved the architecture. The romantic allusions throughout the designs fitted perfectly with his penchant for the nostalgic. Stumbling upon these neglected beauties satisfied his theory that one comes upon the work of the Muse unexpectedly. With characteristic exuberance, he would dash from one building to the next, trying to grasp all of the pleasures available. Barnstone also loved the drama associated with the old wealthy families of Galveston and the leading roles they played in the intrigue of Galveston's economic and political life. For him it was high theater—and it only added to Galveston's allure. Somewhere in those years Barnstone conceived, as his wife recalls, the idea of documenting with photographs and text the architectural treasures he had discovered.[6]

How did the idea for the book come about? Was the idea Barnstone's alone, or did it arise from some sort of joint inspiration involving two other persons: James Johnson Sweeney and Jean de Menil?

James Johnson Sweeney, formerly of the Guggenheim Museum in New York, had become director of the Museum of Fine Arts, Houston, in 1961. A museum press release of June 1962 noted that in the previous year Sweeney had proposed to the museum trustees that the museum initiate a program of publications "with a book on the disappearing architecture of Galveston—the 19th-century architecture principally, which is being demolished so quickly."[7] The museum release went on to state:

We discussed this with Mr. Howard Barnstone, who is an enthusiast for the romantic background for architecture, different revivals, and mixtures of them which are peculiar to Galveston. It was suggested we start with that and we asked him to write the text. He agreed. It was agreed to find photographic documents.[8]

The other key figure in the early planning stage of the book was Jean (John) de Menil. De Menil was president of the Schlumberger Companies and a man of vast financial resources. Perhaps more important, he and his wife, Dominique de Menil, were major art collectors at the center of the international avant-garde and innovators when it came to architectural projects. Barnstone had been introduced to the de Menils by architect Philip Johnson and had later designed several corporate buildings for Schlumberger Companies.[9]

Conceivably, Barnstone lured Sweeney, the de Menils and others to visit Galveston with him, where they were captivated by the architectural spendors of the town. What is absolutely clear is that the book would not have become a reality without the Museum of Fine Arts, Houston, and the personal and financial backing of the de Menils. Evidence exists that Barnstone had, in fact, been looking for project funding for a number of years. In 1960 he was turned down by the Guggenheim and several other foundations.[10] Despite these setbacks, by late 1960 or early 1961, Barnstone had found a backer for the project in Jean de Menil, while the Museum of Fine Arts, Houston, under the new directorship of James Johnson Sweeney, became the organizing entity.[11]

The Photographers

By March 1962 things were moving. The first photographer to be considered for the book was Ezra Stoller. Barnstone had mentioned Stoller, along with G. E. Ridder-Smith, as the kind of first-class architectural photographer that he would want for the book. Now, in an exchange of letters between Barnstone and Stoller, fee and schedule negotiations began in earnest.[12]

Stoller, based in New York, was an architect by training and was known in professional circles as an outstanding architectural photographer. He was much sought after by architectural firms and their clients to present new projects to their best

advantage. He had had a one-man exhibition in the Pepsi-Cola Building in New York, and the Smithsonian Institution routinely circulated displays of his architectural photographs from its permanent collection. In 1961 Stoller had been awarded a gold medal by the American Institute of Architects. Among his clients were leading magazines such as *Vogue, House Beautiful, House & Garden* and *Fortune*.[13]

Yet, other events were already transpiring to preclude Stoller's participation in the project, seemingly forever. Jean de Menil was arranging for the great photographer Henri Cartier-Bresson to work

on the book. And Cartier-Bresson strongly object-
ed to the involvement of any other photographer.[14]

One must be a bit surprised at the choice of
Cartier-Bresson for a book providing documentation and "scholarly research on the great 19th century architecture of Galveston."[15] For this, a photographer such as Stoller would seem a natural—
one would not as readily expect Cartier-Bresson, a
photojournalist and master of the photo portrait.
While it is true that, on occasion, he magnificently
captured the rhythmic and spatial composition of a
particular landscape, one does not find in his *oeuvre*
examples of architectural photography in the clas-
sic sense—that is, carefully balanced images of
individual structures or architectural details. Why
then select Cartier-Bresson?

First, he was a renowned photographer. By
the early 1960s he was among a handful of photographers recognized around the world for their
genius. In 1954 the Louvre in Paris had set aside
a longtime policy against exhibiting photography
by mounting a show of his work. He had published a series of important books, including *The
Decisive Moment* (1952), *The Europeans* (1955),
People of Moscow (1955), *China in Transition* (1956)
and *From One China to Another* (1956). He had won
photographic awards from U.S. *Camera*, the
American Society of Magazine Photographers, the
Photographic Society of America and the
Overseas Press Club.[16] His life represented an
unending quest for expression and communication
through art, his intent invariably being "to seize
the whole essence, in the confines of a single photograph, of some situation that was in the process
of unrolling itself before my eyes."[17] For Cartier-
Bresson, always carrying his Leica camera, it was
a matter of waiting with awareness for what he
called "the decisive moment" of an event or situation, the instant when a particular human expression is at its purest and when the visual composition aligns itself with that emotion.

Without doubt, Cartier-Bresson's participation
in the book would bring a formidable talent to the
project and attract keen interest in photographic
circles and beyond.

As Gertrude Barnstone recalls, her husband
was familiar with Cartier-Bresson's philosophy
and perhaps knew him personally through his own
work in the 1950s and 1960s as editor of *Intercom*,
the international house magazine of the
Schlumberger Companies. Barnstone was on the
cutting edge when it came to graphics and design,
and his wife believes that he was intrigued with
the idea of using Cartier-Bresson, who was so
good at photographing people, to photograph
architecture. It was "an iconoclastic approach,"
but Barnstone thought that it would help people
see the old, neglected buildings in a new way.[18]

The moving force, though, in contacting
Cartier-Bresson, and almost certainly in urging his
selection, was Jean de Menil. The de Menils
knew Cartier-Bresson both professionally and personally. The initial letter from Magnum Photos
regarding Cartier-Bresson's participation in the
project noted that the agreement was based on
conversations between the photographer and Jean
de Menil as well as conversations between Inge
Bondi of Magnum and de Menil.[19]

And why, one asks, would Cartier-Bresson
accept this project, given his multitude of opportunities? The letter from Magnum stated that
Cartier-Bresson "has special regard and affection
for the vitality that he finds in Texas and hopes to
be able to capture in his photographs of Galveston
all the many facets of this town."[20] Probably more
important, however, was the relationship between
Cartier-Bresson and de Menil. As a letter from
Magnum to de Menil stated, "Henri was delighted
to work with you on a project—and he would
never have accepted it, had this idea not come
from you."[21]

Cartier-Bresson arrived in Houston on April 30, 1962 and spent the first two nights at the de Menils' home, thereafter staying as planned at a hotel in Galveston to be closer to his subject and work without interruption.[22]

Gertrude Barnstone remembers Cartier-Bresson, who spoke fluent English, as "very direct and sweet, relating to people immediately." He always started his day by reading poetry to inspire him for the work ahead. He had "a slight touch of courtliness in his manner." She recalls Cartier-Bresson's joy in his work, particularly one morning in Galveston when she, her husband, their two girls and Cartier-Bresson were having breakfast in the hotel coffee shop and Cartier-Bresson started taking photographs of them all simply for the fun of it. Asked if Cartier-Bresson liked Galveston, Gertrude Barnstone recalls that he was "so responsive and perceptive as a person." He loved his surroundings wherever he was and did the same thing in Galveston, "simply eating it up."[23]

Cartier-Bresson was accompanied by Barnstone throughout the assignment, the two men working together in shooting and selecting the pictures.[24] They were assisted by Tom Rice, a local expert on Galveston history and musical director of Trinity Episcopal Church.

At the end of the first week of work, a Sunday afternoon meeting of the Galveston Historical Foundation featured Cartier-Bresson as the honored guest. After attending a small party at the home of Mildred Robertson, a Galveston preservationist, Cartier-Bresson dined with Barnstone. Rice, after the party, went to the bar of the photographer's hotel and waited there for several hours to see if Cartier-Bresson, on his return, would join him for further conversation. In going to the men's room, Rice opened the wrong door, which, incredibly, opened onto nothing. He fell two stories and died soon afterward, despite extensive surgery. As Gertrude Barnstone recalls, Cartier-Bresson was devastated and felt in some way responsible for not having joined Rice in the bar, thus, perhaps, preventing the bizarre tragedy.[25]

Cartier-Bresson went on to complete ten days of photographing as planned. His photographs of Galveston show the architectural beauty of the old city's structures, many of which are worn, even dilapidated. There is a sense of slowness about everything, communicated most effectively, often brilliantly, in those images in which people are the central feature, with the structure providing their context. In the photos of buildings without people, the viewer is treated to full shots that often include foliage as well as to images involving unusual perspectives designed to capture the complex angles and fanciful millwork of the buildings.

In one of Cartier-Bresson's photographs of the Voelcker House (page 88), a major column of the galleries aligns itself with the overlapping torsos of two men in the foreground. These figures, one leaning and one walking, give the impression of a neighborhood slowly dying. Of similar impact is the photograph "Vernacular Greek Houses, Avenue I" (page 40) in which the porch, with its columns, heavy railing and balusters, forms with the façade of the house a framework for three men sprawled on a battered couch. In a less-dramatic but beautifully done photo of the Washington Hotel (page 35), an elderly proprietress steadies herself on the gracefully curved banister, one of many people of moderate means making do in these structures that were once the grandest in Texas. The beautiful curve of the shining banister railing relates the two rectangular surfaces of light-covered walls separated by the blackness of the hall opening.

A number of other photographs gain their power from a combination of people and historical structures. A photograph of Congregation B'nai Israel Synagogue (pages 74–75) includes a solitary person set against the massive façade of the former synagogue and stark cement paving of the parking lot. In a photograph of the Block-Oppenheimer Building (page 80), two figures, both neatly dressed, stoop in the doorway of a Strand building as if to be shielded from the bright sun. And a photograph of the Sonnentheil House (pages

152–53) juxtaposes both the lovely white millwork of this frame house and the gnarled live oaks with the figure of a man in loose work clothes, in the lower left foreground.

Delightful contrasts to these stolid figures are the children captured with their energy and playfulness—for example, the young boy with his package racing across the street in "Congregation B'nai Israel Synagogue" (page 76) and the girl running up the front steps of the Sawyer-Flood House (page 93). Another interesting image is the one of Sacred Heart Church (pages 192–93) in which a man stands respectfully, holding his hat, before the magnificent symmetrical church façade. A large supporting column runs from bottom to top in the exact middle of the photo, centering everything in a beautiful interplay of person, building and intricate shadows.

Cartier-Bresson also took a large number of photographs without people that highlighted a par-ticular portion of a structure or presented it as a whole. In doing this, he often utilized an unexpected angle, a stimulating interplay among the lines of the structure or a contrast with the irregular curves or softness of live oaks, palms or other foliage. Examples include his images of the McDonald House (frontispiece), the Brown House (page 52) and the Austin-Fox House (pages 68–69).

What do we know about Cartier-Bresson's impression of Galveston? The few remaining records are telling. Several days after leaving Galveston, he wrote to de Menil, saying, "I believe that the better way to tell you what I think will be to do a book on Galveston that expresses the strange and ephemeral life of this butterfly of the 19th century."[26] And, in response to a 1988 letter from me, Cartier-Bresson wrote, "I hope that my photographs . . . have been able to transmit the elegance, the charm, the rigor of this architecture representing a world which, unhappily, has disappeared."[27]

Ezra Stoller in Galveston

Something was brewing, however. It appears that questions were being raised as to whether or not Cartier-Bresson's photographs gave complete enough coverage for the purpose of the book. The first indication of such a concern is a letter written in October 1962 to Barnstone from Frank A. Wardlaw, then director of the University of Texas Press. He expressed strong interest in the book but added,

My only reservation about it is the feeling that there aren't enough of the Cartier-Bresson photographs and that they do not really adequately represent the "architectural" exuberance of Galveston.[28]

Wardlaw must have raised a doubt shared by Barnstone and at least acknowledged by Sweeney and de Menil. Barnstone responded to Wardlaw that the original plan had been to have Ezra Stoller do a portion of the photographs,[29] and on that same day, he wrote to Stoller, beginning his letter, "Man, this is a difficult one to write." Barnstone updated Stoller on the book's progress and asked him to consider rejoining the project.[30]

Meanwhile, it is likely, as Dominique de Menil recalls, that her husband was trying to get Cartier-Bresson to agree to the addition of Stoller. In any case, Barnstone was able to write Stoller on November 28 that over coffee in New York, Cartier-Bresson had agreed "from the point of view of the book that his coverage was incomplete and further agreed that you would be the architectural photographer as originally planned."[31]

Things were worked out with Stoller, who recalls that he decided to set aside his pride and once again accept the assignment.[32] Thus, in March 1963, he spent nine days in Galveston photographing and sent Barnstone 123 prints by the end of that month. He returned briefly to Galveston in April to shoot some interiors.

Stoller notes that he was trained in architecture in the late 1930s, when the influence of the Beaux

Arts school was fading and modern architecture, with its emphasis on functionalism, was being embraced. For Stoller this meant, among other things, an assignment-oriented photography rather than the creation of art as a goal in itself.

In the case of the Galveston assignment, however, he set aside looking at the historical structures in terms of twentieth-century functionalism. He sought to see the structures as they were used and viewed in the nineteenth century by the people building and residing in them. In doing this, he was especially interested in those photographs that gave a sense of space around the structures or a sense of the relationship of the structures to each other and the way they were a part of the city.[33]

Stoller's photographs are crucial to the presentation of Galveston architecture in the book. While they may appear to be straightforward shots, they usually involve more subtlety of angle and composition than first meets the eye. In total, they provide a foundation of excellent architectural coverage upon which the more interpretive, people-oriented photos of Cartier-Bresson build. Some of them are masterpieces of architectural photography.

A number of Stoller's photographs are straight-on shots of the entire façade of an important structure and its setting—for example, his photograph of the Menard House (pages 10–11), which shows the structure exactly centered in the frame. The large live oaks play against the strong vertical and horizontal lines of the nearly symmetrical façade, the intricate leaves and shadows adding softness and complexity. In other photographs, Stoller employs an unusual angle in such a natural way that the viewer does not notice—for example, the images of the Williams-Tucker House (page 14), the Sealy House (page 169) and, especially, the Lasker House (page 176).

Stoller was equally adept at capturing the architectural character and relationships of a row of houses, whether with a straight-on shot, such as the one of the vernacular Greek houses on Avenue I (pages 42–43), or with an angle shot, such as his photograph of the Reymershoffer House (page 199), which creates a series of spatial relationships among structures by capturing the porch of one house, the street in front and, across the street, two fine Victorian houses on corner lots.

Frequently Stoller shifts from his straight-on approach to capture the particular beauty of an individual structure. His treatment of the Darragh House, for example, involves the usual, competent, straight-on shot (page 141) as well as a seductive composition evoking romantic Galveston (page 144). One of his photographs of the Gresham House may at first appear to be a bit too artistic, but it in fact captures the intimate proximity of smaller, simpler structures to the ornate mansion to create a single architectural massing (pages 164–65).

The Photographs Together

On the whole, the distinctive approaches of Stoller and Cartier-Bresson provide a wonderful counterpoint that strengthens and enriches the presentation of each structure. Most delightful are the photographs of Sacred Heart Church and the Lucas Apartments. Concerning Sacred Heart, Stoller provided a strong image of the entire façade (page 190). Cartier-Bresson's photograph follows, the magnificent shot of the double portals with the standing worshipper (pages 192–93). For the Lucas Apartments, Stoller provided an excellent full-façade photograph taken at an angle (page 203), while Cartier-Bresson's image of the same apartments (page 204) is a straight-on shot of a portion of the façade, made intricate with playing shadows and the pattern of a barren tree. Given the wonderful counterpoint between the work of the two artists, it is interesting to note that neither saw the photographs of the other during the project.[34]

No commentary on the photographs in the book would be complete without special mention of the fine historical photographs included from the archives of the Rosenberg Library, Galveston. These are essential in depicting one-time landmarks, such as the Beach Hotel, lost around 1898, and the Ursuline Academy, lost after hurricane Carla. They are also marvelous in showing landmarks prior to extensive renovations, such as the Congregation B'nai Israel Synagogue.

In addition, the book includes a number of excellent contemporary pen-and-ink drawings by Houston artist Robert Kendrick to lend further interpretation to several of the major structures. The text represents massive amounts of research by Barnstone and others at the Rosenberg Library and elsewhere, serving as a solid companion to the photographs.

Publishing the Book

As early as August 1962, soon after Cartier-Bresson's visit, Barnstone began looking for a publisher for the book. By May 1963 he was proposing a joint publication/distribution arrangement between the University of Texas Press and Yale University Press, while the former was pressing hard to be the sole publisher and distributor—albeit contingent upon seeing a completed manuscript.[35]

In November Barnstone submitted an initial draft of the text to Yale, but the press found it insufficiently scholarly for publication.[36] He then submitted it to the Macmillan Company,[37] though the University of Texas Press continued to express strong interest and asked several times to see the draft manuscript.[38] A letter confirms, however, that by February 1964 Barnstone and Sweeney had concluded that they preferred a non-university press.[39]

In June 1964 Macmillan and the museum signed a publishing contract for the book.[40] All through that fall and the following spring, the editing of the text, photographs and illustrations continued, with Barnstone objecting unsuccessfully to

"wholesale cutting" of particular quotes and the cutting of the original Nicholas Clayton drawings.[41] Macmillan set an official publication date of January 1966.[42]

More than three years before the book was published, Barnstone had already begun a campaign to publicize the project and draw the public's attention to Galveston's unique architecture. Within a few weeks of the museum's June 1962 announcement of the project, he was being interviewed by the *Galveston Daily News*. He continued to speak on the subject, warning that Galveston was in danger of losing much of its historic architecture, with many historic buildings already torn down to make room for newer structures.[43]

When release of the book was imminent, a gala opening was held at the Museum of Fine Arts, Houston, on November 30, 1965, to preview the photographs of Cartier-Bresson and Stoller and to view copies of the book itself, tightly sealed in a glass case. The first book signing was held on December 19 at Trinity Church in Galveston, with more than three hundred persons attending. It was a sell-out.

Reception of the Book

Critical reaction to the book was virtually all favorable, even glowing. The *Houston Chronicle* called the photographs "distinguished indeed" and

the text "a pleasant account" with "a fairly painless discussion" of the architecture.[44] The *Houston Post* reviewer loved the book, calling it "rare and different . . . exceptionally beautiful. But it is also intelligent, literate, perceptive and informative."[45] The *Dallas Morning News* review called it "an amazing book, certainly one of the most welcome and most solid pieces of Texana in this century."[46]

In March 1966 came a review in the *New York Times* that called the book "handsome" and the photographs "distinguished."[47] Beyond that, the review focused not on the book but rather on the book's message: the rise and fall of Galveston, the exuberant architecture and its current destruction.

The most provocative review, and Barnstone's favorite, was in the *Dallas Times Herald*. The reviewer found Barnstone expressing the reviewer's own feeling that

> Galveston is a city which died in 1900. What remains in my memory is a sort of Texas Camelot, entirely more enchanting than any real city because it is a place of the mind where imperfection is repaired by imagination . . . a city which does not exist, if it ever did exist; a place of the past whose real history was its spirit.[48]

The review sensed the "brooding or fanciful" feeling of the book—fanciful in that the reader was being shown a Victorian city arrested in time, without the day-to-day life of that time. Rather, the book evokes the spirit of the city from the romanticism of its architecture. The brooding, too, is there in the book—the nagging yet never adequately answered question of why this grandeur failed to flourish beyond its Victorian heyday. One dreams that this graceful Camelot of a city might have prevailed, but, in reality, dynamic growth and the romantic Victorian architecture in such a confined land area would have been incompatible in the first half of this century. Ironically, Galveston's failed economic expansion was the very reason that the marvelous structures of its past glory managed to survive.

The issue of historic preservation was best raised, appropriately enough, in the extensive review of the book in *Historic Preservation* magazine, published by the National Trust for Historic Preservation. Here, reviewer James C. Massey of

the Historic American Buildings Survey warmly praised the "thoroughly professional" quality of the text and photography and concluded that it "set an enviable model for other cities to follow in documenting their own historic heritage." More important, he suggested the book would "do much to boost the significance of Galveston's historic landmarks and to create the favorable public attitudes and interest essential for a successful community preservation program."[49]

In fact, even though Galveston gave the book a favorable reception, there were undercurrents of dissatisfaction. For one, some leading Galvestonians felt that the photographs by Cartier-Bresson seemed to focus on run-down, even derelict, neighborhoods and houses. These were strong images, and they tended to influence a reading of the book as a whole. Some people were thus offended that a community they loved had been presented, in their opinion, in an unfavorable light.[50]

A second source of dissatisfaction was that Barnstone, in his introduction to the book, blamed Galveston's leaders at the turn of the century for the city's loss of commercial momentum, and the ascendancy of Houston. He claimed that those leaders simply did not want the city to grow, though he admitted that the charge could not be documented. It was true that an objective answer as to why Houston rather than Galveston became a major city of the twentieth century would require extensive research; yet, the undocumented charge was made, and the response from leading Galveston families was one of hurt and anger.[51]

A third negative reaction was to Barnstone's blitz of press conferences and speaking engagements in which he suggested ways to breathe new economic life into the old structures. The immediate reaction was polite disinterest. The *Galveston Daily News* praised Barnstone as a brilliant architect and artist but contrasted his ideas with those of "a realistic businessman and city builder" who would be sure that Galveston did not miss the boat of economic greatness again. Saving historic structures, it was believed, was not relevant to the city's future.[52]

The book and Barnstone's preservation ideas were, nevertheless, filtering through the Galveston community. As Tim Thompson, an early Galveston preservationist, recalls:

The book taught that the trend was downwards and nothing was around to restrain the inevitable demolitions. Barnstone did not say that, but Galvestonians knew it was true. Something caused them to wake up and listen to those who were talking preservation, and Barnstone should get a prize for being, if not all of it, the biggest piece of the wakeup call.[53]

One group responding to the call was the Junior League of Galveston. In 1968 the League singlehandedly saved the Trueheart-Adriance Building from destruction and focused attention on the importance of saving the historic Strand commercial area as a whole. In a separate effort in 1968, individual preservationists saved the west section of the 1859 Hendley Row from demolition—the windows already having been torn out—and donated it to the Galveston Historical Foundation. And in 1969 the Texas Historical Commission successfully nominated the Strand for listing on the National Register of Historic Places.

Meanwhile, in 1967 the Galveston Historical Foundation, with backing from the Moody Foundation, had initiated an extensive architectural survey of the city. In early 1970 they succeeded in having forty blocks of the residential East End designated an historic district, with city veto power over demolitions and exterior changes to structures. In addition, the Harris and Eliza Kempner Fund initiated a program of low-interest loans for the rehabilitation of historic houses there.

Most indicative that the wake-up call had been heard, however, was the 1969–74 struggle to save and restore the 1859 Italianate J. M. Brown House, or "Ashton Villa." The landmark's owners had appraisals showing the land worth more without the structure than with it and threatened demolition unless their price was met. In an unprecedented and perhaps illegal action, the Galveston City Council passed an ordinance forbidding demolition of Ashton Villa and four other antebellum structures. Agreement on a compromise price was soon reached, and after more years of work to restore and furnish the landmark, it was opened to the public as a museum.

In 1972 representatives of the Moody Foundation, the Kempner Fund, the Cultural Arts Council and the Historical Foundation initiated the Strand Revolving Fund. The fund's purpose was to enable the Galveston Historical Foundation to purchase Strand buildings, place protective deed restrictions on them and attract investors to buy and rehabilitate them for active uses.

As a young lawyer and neophyte preservationist recruited to organize the Strand effort and serve as executive director of the Galveston Historical Foundation, I was shown *The Galveston That Was* and can recall still how much I liked the book and the legitimacy it gave to the urgency and importance of saving the city's historic structures. It was only years later that I realized it was also planned as a requiem: a final recording before inevitable destruction.

Perhaps this part of the book's meaning was obscured by the beauty of the structures brought together and presented so intensely: one saw them and immediately assumed that there had to be some way to save them. Then, too, forces in the community had changed enough by the 1970s that the desire to save them had become a call to action with a realistic chance of success. Barnstone himself was usually nearby with his unflagging enthusiasm and support for preserving Galveston's historical structures, efforts that were redoubled once he found like-minded allies.

Since the early 1970s much has been accomplished by the Galveston community, with support from Houston and around the state. Some forty historic buildings in the Strand area have been restored, and the area is now designated a National Historic Landmark and protected by the creation of a local historic district. An estimated two million people annually frequent the seventy or so shops, restaurants and galleries. The First National Bank Building is now an arts center, the Hendley Building houses a busy visitor's center, and the old Santa Fe Building is a major railroad museum with excursion trains running from Houston. The Strand is complemented by a revitalized waterfront, with the restored 1877 barque *Elissa*, the Texas Seaport Museum and other public uses. South of the Strand is the Grand Opera House, now an elegant performing arts center, and the County Historical Museum is housed in the 1906 Moody Building. These areas are again linked to the beachfront with a fixed-rail trolley system, and two major events—Dickens on the Strand and Mardi Gras—entertain more than five hundred thousand persons annually.

The Ashbel Smith Building ("Old Red") at the University of Texas Medical School, once threatened with demolition, has been restored and is again a central part of the school. Nearby, the East End is largely intact as one of the loveliest Victorian residential areas in the nation. And the famous Gresham House, called the "Bishop's Palace," is open to the public as a house museum.

In the central part of the city, the Brown House still graces Broadway as a fine house museum, the Sealy House is being restored by the University of Texas Medical Branch and the nearby Willis-Moody House has been restored as a museum. The fifteen-block Silk Stocking District has been established, and the Powhattan Hotel is maintained by the Galveston Garden Club. Nearby, the Williams-Tucker House is restored and open as an interpretive center. The Menard House, long deteriorating in the hands of speculators, has been rescued by the Galveston Historical Foundation and is now in the process of being restored by new owners.

Crucial to this restoration effort is the moral and financial support of the old Galveston and Houston families and developers such as George and Cynthia Mitchell, who are committed to quality restoration and volunteer leadership. At present the linchpin of much of this work is the hundreds of thousands of visitors who now come to historic Galveston. Other job opportunities for Galveston residents would help shore up the economic base to restore and maintain the nearly two thousand structures already identified.

Despite this major turnaround in Galveston's commitment to preserve its historic structures and ambiance, it is still painful to look through *The Galveston That Was* and see what has been lost. Five of the loveliest structures, including the Beach Hotel, had been lost in the 1800s, or well prior to the book. More major buildings were lost from 1962 to 1965, while the book was actually in process. Among these, the loss of the Ursuline Academy is enough to drive a preservationist crazy, not to mention Henry's Bookstore and the Salvation Army Building. Soon after the publication of the book, the Voelcker House and the Lasker House were demolished, and the façade of the Galveston News Building was covered over.

Yet, one must remember that a large number of the structures featured in the book stand intact today. None have been lost through outright demolition since 1970. Three important ones, however, have been largely destroyed by fire and then demolished: the Heidenheimer Castle, the Darragh House and the Washington Hotel, though the last has been miraculously restored and reconstructed by George and Cynthia Mitchell. (The loss of the Darragh House is especially painful, given the many years of community fundraising that went into preserving it.)

None of this would have happened without *The Galveston That Was*. Everyone who cares about and enjoys historic Galveston today is indebted to Howard Barnstone and his allies Jean de Menil and James Johnson Sweeney. While the book was insufficient in itself to create this historical renaissance in Galveston, its elegant presentation of the beauty of these historic structures was a necessary and crucial part in awakening Galveston, as well as Houston, to the Victorian treasure that stands on this barrier island. Planned as a requiem, the book has served as the primary inspiration for saving the historic architecture that it documented.

—Peter H. Brink
1993

Notes

1. A number of questions about the book had always intrigued me. How had this special book come to be? How was the unusual combination of photography by Henri Cartier-Bresson and Ezra Stoller conceived? What was the artistic and professional approach of each? How was the book received initially, and what was its eventual impact on Galveston? The excellent files in the archives of the Museum of Fine Arts, Houston (referred to hereafter as "MFA Archives"), and Barnstone's own files in the archives at the Houston Public Library provided a wealth of letters and other documents to help in the search for answers to these questions. In addition, the generous assistance of many of Barnstone's friends and colleagues has been invaluable. Reference books from the Rosenberg Library in Galveston were crucial to my understanding of Cartier-Bresson. And in all of this, I was aided by the fine work of my volunteer research associate and friend, Betty Hartman, of Galveston. The original paper, prepared for the North American Print Conference in November 1988, was dedicated to Howard Barnstone. It will be included in *Prints and Printmakers of Texas: Proceedings of the Twentieth Annual North American Print Conference*, edited by Ron Tyler of the Texas State Historical Association.

2. Historical facts in the previous paragraphs are drawn from or confirmed by David G. McComb, *Galveston: A History* (Austin: University of Texas Press, 1986).

3. Records of the Galveston Historical Foundation, Galveston, Texas.

4. *Galveston Daily News*, 2 February 1962; 11 February 1962; 17 February 1962.

5. *Galveston Daily News*, 17 November 1963; 24 November 1963.

6. The previous paragraphs about Barnstone are based on my interview with Gertrude Barnstone, 11 October 1988.

7. Press release, Museum of Fine Arts, Houston, 13 June 1962, MFA Archives.

8. Ibid.

9. Ann Holmes, "Tour a Tribute to the Magic of Howard Barnstone," *Houston Chronicle Zest*, 23 October 1988. According to Holmes, *Houston Chronicle* fine arts editor, in her 1988 feature story about Barnstone, "A trip to Galveston with the de Menils in the early '50s was the source of Barnstone's later decision to write the book *The Galveston That Was*."

10. In a letter to the secretary of the Guggenheim Foundation, dated 9 February 1960, Barnstone mentioned a lunch with a Dr. Alfred Frankfurter and the de Menils: "I was talking with Dr. Frankfurter and told him of my hopes to do a scholarly, yet, at the same time lively research project on the fast disappearing romantic architecture in Galveston. Dr. Frankfurter at once suggested that I write to you, outlining the program, and indicating that he had suggested that I write. What I need is about $5,000–$6,000 to help pay for the cost of preparing measured drawings, a research assistant, and photographs. I had planned for the program to take from 9 to 12 months and hoped for eventual publication. The only existing description of Galveston's early architecture is a little 20-page pamphlet put out by the ladies of the local historical society." (H. Barnstone to Dr. Henry A. Moe, secretary, John Simon Guggenheim Memorial Foundation, New York, 9 February 1960, Howard Barnstone Files, Archives, Houston Public Library) See also Mrs. Josephine Leighton, administrative assistant, Guggenheim Foundation, to H. Barnstone, 11 February 1960; and H. Barnstone to Mrs. Leighton, 16 February 1960. See also Mrs. Leighton to H. Barnstone, 19 February 1960; H. Barnstone to Mrs. Leighton, 23 February 1960; and Mrs. Leighton to H. Barnstone 26 February 1960; Howard Barnstone Files, Archives, Houston Public Library.

Barnstone was also writing to Mrs. E. Clyde Northen, a member of the Moody family and trustee of the Moody Foundation. "What I have in mind is the eventual publication of a definitive book with photographs, plans and historic details of all the major buildings." In addition, he states that he would use "a first class architectural photographer, such as G.E. Ridder-Smith or Ezra Stoller, for existing buildings." (H. Barnstone to Mrs. E. Clyde Northen, Galveston, 23 February 1960, Howard Barnstone Files, Archives, Houston Public Library)

The secretary of the Moody Foundation responded by advising Barnstone that "the Trust Indenture of The Moody Foundation does not allow for such a contribution as requested." Presumably, this was a reference to the foundation's policy of not making grants to individuals. (A. T. Whayne, secretary of the Moody Foundation, to H. Barnstone, 17 March 1960, Howard Barnstone Files, Archives, Houston Public Library)

11. Interview with Gertrude Barnstone, 11 October 1988, and with Dominique de Menil, 6 October 1988. See also James Sweeney to Jean de Menil, 25 May 1962, MFA Archives. A letter of 15 January 1965 from de Menil to Sweeney notes that the de Menils had contributed some $20,000 to make the book possible.

12. H. Barnstone to Ezra Stoller, 13 and 23 March 1962; Ezra Stoller to H. Barnstone, 21 March 1962, MFA Archives.

13. Advertisement for *The Galveston That Was*, Museum of Fine Arts, Houston (self mailer).

14. Among other letters, James Sweeney to Miss Inge Bondi, Magnum Photos, 16 April 1962, MFA Archives. On May 18 Barnstone wrote Stoller what he described as "one of the most difficult letters I have ever had to write." (H. Barnstone to Ezra Stoller, 18 May 1962, MFA Archives). Noting that "the book was to have been a collaborative effort on the part of yourself [Stoller] as well as subjective photographs," he further stated that they had finally settled on Cartier-Bresson, who had recently visited Galveston. Barnstone continued:

> The problem that has now come up is that he, Cartier-Bresson, feels that he has given adequate coverage and doesn't want another photographer to be involved. He has made this point very strongly to me and to Jim Sweeney, Director of the Museum who is the publisher, and to John de Menil who is the backer.
>
> In view of the hesitation you indicated in your note of 28th April, would it be better if we dropped the idea of the documentary photographs and let Cartier-Bresson have his way?

Stoller responded: "Sorry you had to be the axe

but if Bresson has done it, it is done and I'll just change my plans and cancel the trip." (Ezra Stoller to H. Barnstone, 21 May 1962, MFA Archives)

15. H. Barnstone to Mrs. E. Clyde Northen, 23 February 1960, MFA Archives.

16. Charles Moritz, ed., *Current Biography* (New York: H.W. Wilson, 1976), 81–82.

17. Henri Cartier-Bresson, *The Decisive Moment* (New York: Simon & Schuster, 1952), 2.

18. Interview with Gertrude Barnstone, 11 October 1988. James Johnson Sweeney, in an MFA press release, stated, "We felt that we might work with documents from the library but in the end decided that it would be interesting to have one of the finest contemporary photographers to work on it—someone who had a sympathy with the romantic background of the material. Mr. Cartier-Bresson's name was proposed to Mr. Barnstone and the Trustees." (Press release, Museum of Fine Arts, Houston, 13 June 1962, MFA Archives)

19. Gedeon de Margitay, Magnum Photos, to H. Barnstone, 13 April 1962, MFA Archives. Indeed, in a recent letter, 5 October 1988, from Cartier-Bresson to myself, he stated, "The idea of the book *The Galveston That Was* comes from Jean and Dominique de Menil who, with their enthusiasm and their usual generosity, have enabled the idea to be realized, with the aid of our friend, architect Howard Barnstone."

20. Ibid.

21. Miss Inge Bondi, Magnum Photos, to Jean de Menil, 7 June 1962, MFA Archives. This is further evidenced by Cartier-Bresson's initial willingness to undertake the ten-day assignment for the surprisingly low fee of $2,000 plus expenses from New York, with no additional royalties, proceeding on the basis solely of verbal understandings and a one-page letter.

22. Gedeon de Margitay, Magnum Photos, to H. Barnstone, 24 April 1962, MFA Archives.

23. Interview with Gertrude Barnstone, 11 October 1988.

24. Miss Inge Bondi, Magnum Photos, to H. Barnstone, 7 June 1962.

25. Interview with Gertrude Barnstone, 11 October 1988.

26. Henri Cartier-Bresson to Jean de Menil, 15 May 1962, MFA Archives.

27. Henri Cartier-Bresson to Peter Brink, 5 October 1988.

28. Frank H. Wardlaw, director, University of Texas

Press, to H. Barnstone, 2 October 1962, MFA Archives.

29. H. Barnstone to Frank H. Wardlaw, 3 October 1962, MFA Archives.

30. H. Barnstone to Ezra Stoller, 3 October 1962, MFA Archives. In the letter, Barnstone elaborated:

> As you see from the Texas letter, the weakness of a book with only Cartier-Bresson photographs, which I had fully anticipated in my preliminary talks with you, have now become a factor in the position of the publishers and providing we can chain Cartier-Bresson to a stake somewhere in Tibet with a hand-knitted muffler wound five times around his head, would you under any circumstances be willing to come back in the picture and do what you and I had talked of over a year ago?

31. H. Barnstone to Ezra Stoller, 28 November 1962, MFA Archives.

32. Interview with Ezra Stoller, 9 November 1988.

33. The previous paragraphs are based on my interview with Ezra Stoller, 9 November 1988.

34. Ibid.

35. H. Barnstone to Chester Rerr, director, Yale University Press, 28 May 1963. See also Frank H. Wardlaw, to H. Barnstone, 1 November 1963, MFA Archives.

36. Chester Rerr to H. Barnstone, 20 November 1963, MFA Archives.

37. H. Barnstone to Cecil Scott, executive editor, Macmillan Company, 5 December 1963; Cecil Scott, to H. Barnstone, 3 January 1964; and H. Barnstone to Cecil Scott, 9 January 1964, MFA Archives.

38. Frank H. Wardlaw to H. Barnstone, 1 November 1963, 26 November 1963 and 13 January 1964, MFA Archives.

39. H. Barnstone to Henri Cartier-Bresson, 6 February 1964, MFA Archives.

40. Agreement, Museum of Fine Arts, Houston, and Macmillan Company, 16 June 1964, MFA Archives.

41. H. Barnstone to James Sweeney, 30 April 1965, MFA Archives.

42. Cecil Scott to H. Barnstone, 3 November 1965, MFA Archives.

43. *Galveston Daily News*, 22 December 1964.

44. *Houston Chronicle*, 12 December 1965.

45. *Houston Post*, 19 December 1965.

46. *Dallas Morning News*, 26 December 1965.

47. *New York Times Book Review*, 6 March 1966.

48. *Dallas Times Herald*, 2 January 1966.

49. James C. Massey, book review, *Historic Preservation* (January/February 1966): 38, 41.

50. *Galveston Gazette*, 3 February 1966; interview with Mildred Robertson, 28 September 1988; interview with Edward R. ("Tim") Thompson, Jr., 22 October 1988; and interview with E. Burke Evans, 5 October 1988.

51. Interview with Edward R. ("Tim") Thompson, Jr., 2 October 1988.

52. *Galveston Daily News*, 31 January 1966, editorial.

53. Edward R. ("Tim") Thompson, Jr., to Peter Brink, 4 October 1988.

Index